To Prefer Nothing to Christ

To Prefer Nothing to CHRIST

The Monastic Mission of the English Benedictine Congregation

An English Benedictine Statement
in the Year of Consecrated Life, 2015

Foreword by
Abbot John Klassen, OSB

LITURGICAL PRESS

Collegeville, Minnesota

www.litpress.org

Cover design by Monica Bokinskie. Photo: English Benedictine Extraordinary Chapter Meeting at Buckfast Abbey, July 26th until July 29th, 2015. Used with permission.

© 2016 by Order of Saint Benedict, Collegeville, Minnesota. All rights reserved. No part of this book may be reproduced in any form, by print, microfilm, microfiche, mechanical recording, photocopying, translation, or by any other means, known or yet unknown, for any purpose except brief quotations in reviews, without the previous written permission of Liturgical Press, Saint John's Abbey, PO Box 7500, Collegeville, Minnesota 56321-7500. Printed in the United States of America.

Library of Congress Control Number: 2016943911

ISBN 978-0-8146-4620-5   978-0-8146-4646-5 (ebook)

CONTENTS

Foreword: Abbot John Klassen, OSB   ix

Introduction: Called and Chosen [§§ 1–10]   1

Chapter One:
Monastic CONSECRATION in the English Congregation [§§ 11–37]   11

The Word who calls [§§ 13–14]   13

Encounter and journey with Jesus [§§ 15–17]   13

Encountering Jesus in monastic community [§§ 18–19]   15

Spiritual paternity [§§ 20–23]   16

Formation and growth to our full stature in Christ [§§ 24–27]   20

Monastic profession [§§ 28–32]   23

Evangelical counsels, evangelical lives [§§ 33–37]   25

Chapter Two:
Monastic COMMUNION in the English Congregation [§§ 38–89]   29

Part 1: A theology of monastic communion [§§ 41–51]   31

Church and monastery as communion [§§ 41–43]   31

Monastic communion reflects the life of the holy Trinity in the Church [§§ 44–46]   33

Monastic communion as a fruit of the resurrection of Jesus [§§ 47–48]   35

Monastic communion and sharing in the self-emptying of Christ [§§ 49–51]   36

Part 2: A school of communion [§ 52–76]   38

The daily experience of monastic communion [§§ 53–57]   38

Supporting monastic communion [§§ 58–67]   41
    Leadership in promoting monastic communion [§§ 59–61]   41
    Consultation, decision, discernment [§§ 62–64]   43
    Monastic enclosure [§§ 65–67]   44

Nourishing monastic communion [§§ 68–76]   46
    Eucharist and Liturgy of the Hours [§ 69]   46
    Lectio divina *and personal prayer* [§§ 70–72]   47
    Praying at all times; praying for all people [§ 73]   48
    A contemplative life in communion [§§ 74–76]   49

Part 3: Monastic integrity and communion [§§ 77–86]   50

Part 4: Communion and solidarity in the EBC [§§ 87–89]   55

Chapter Three:
Monastic COMMISSION in the English Congregation [§§ 90–133]   57

Monastic consecration for the sake of mission [§§ 95–100]   60

Monastic communion for the sake of mission [§§ 101–4]   64

Mission and the work of the monastery [§§ 105–28]   67
    Monastic hospitality as a means of evangelisation [§§ 112–14]   70
    The monastery within the local church [§§ 115–16]   73

Pastoral mission and English Benedictine monasticism
[§§ 117–21]   74
Educational mission and English Benedictine monasticism
[§§ 122–28]   76

Source and summit of monastic life [§§ 129–33]   82

Afterword: To Wake Up the World [§§ 134–38]   85

References Used in the Statement   89

Index of References to the Bible and the Rule   93

Thematic Index   97

FOREWORD

In 2015 the English congregation of Benedictines commissioned five monastic men and women to draft a statement on "the monastic identity of the English Benedictine Congregation" in response to the Year of Consecrated Life. The result, *To Prefer Nothing to Christ*, will be an exceptional tool for all monastic leaders and those involved in formation and vocation ministry. Titled after a favorite Benedictine quotation from chapter 72 of the Rule of Benedict, the writers take skillful advantage of a beloved gospel passage for monastics: the Lucan account of the encounter of two disciples with the Risen Christ on the road to Emmaus. This scriptural lens provides a way to reflect on a theology of monastic communion flowing out of the self-emptying and resurrection of Christ and the lived experience of communion with Christ and one's fellow monastics in the spiritual practices of Benedictine life. Finally, the authors ground the prayer, apostolic work, and life of each individual monastic and the community in the monastic consecration to and communion with Christ.

This is a rich, nourishing, and fresh integration of the monastic call, using the resources of recent papal teaching (Popes John Paul II, Benedict XVI, and Francis) as well as developments in Christology, ecclesiology, trinitarian theology, and missiology.

Abbot John Klassen, OSB
Saint John's Abbey
Collegeville, Minnesota

INTRODUCTION

Called and Chosen

> Jesus, at the Last Supper, turns to the Apostles with these words: 'You did not choose me, but I chose you' (Jn 15.16). They remind us all . . . that vocation is always an initiative of God. It is Christ who called you to follow him in the consecrated life and this means continuously making an 'exodus' from yourselves in order to centre your life on Christ and on his Gospel, on the will of God, laying aside your own plans, in order to say with St Paul: 'It is no longer I who live, but Christ who lives in me'.[1]

1. 'You did not choose me, but I chose you' (Jn 15.16). These words of Jesus Christ, the Lord who is 'seeking His workman in a multitude of people' (RB Prol.14), have been addressed personally to each one of us. The starting point of our lives as monks and nuns of the English Benedictine Congregation 'is the Word of God, a Word who calls, who invites, who personally summons' (OL 10). It is in response to this personal and originating call of Jesus that we seek,

---

[1] Francis, *Address to the participants at the Plenary Assembly of the International Union of Superiors General*, Rome, 8 May 2013.

like all who live the monastic life, to 'live in a particularly radical way, through monastic profession, the demands flowing from baptismal participation in the Paschal Mystery of Christ's Death and Resurrection';[2] that is to say, to 'prefer nothing whatever to Christ' (RB 72.11).

2. Especially in this Year of Consecrated Life, monks and nuns recognise that 'following Christ, as proposed in the Gospel, is the "ultimate norm of religious life" and the "supreme rule" of all the Institutes. One of the earliest names for monastic life is *evangelical life*'.[3] In order to follow Jesus Christ in monastic life, we have set ourselves to 'Listen carefully [. . .] to the master's instructions' (RB Prol.1). With Pope Benedict XVI, we recognise that when monks and nuns live in the manner to which we have been called 'monasticism can constitute for all the forms of religious life and consecrated life a remembrance of what is essential and has primacy in the life of every baptized person: *to seek Christ and put nothing before his love*'.[4] This English Benedictine Statement of monastic and missionary identity aims to express the central features of our evan-

---

[2] John Paul II, *Vita Consecrata* (=VC), 6.

[3] Congregation for Institutes of Consecrated Life and Societies of Apostolic Life (=CICLSAL), *Keep Watch! Letter to Consecrated Men and Women Journeying in the Footsteps of God* (=KW), 8.

[4] Benedict XVI, *Address to the Plenary Assembly of the Congregation for Consecrated Life and Societies of Apostolic Life* (=Plenary CICLSAL).

gelical way of living for the monks and nuns of our Congregation today.

3. Pope Francis has said of those who live out a vocation in which we prefer nothing to Jesus Christ and his love that 'In calling you, God says to you: "You are important to me, I love you, I am counting on you." Jesus says this to each one of us! Joy is born from that! The joy of the moment in which Jesus looked at me. Understanding and hearing this is the secret of our joy'.[5] To know that we are entrusted with such a profound treasure by the Lord who calls us should indeed be the source of a deep Gospel joy to each monk and nun; at the same time we remain children of Adam and Eve, and 'we hold this treasure in pots of earthenware' (2 Cor 4.7). We are painfully aware that what Pope John Paul II termed 'sad situations of crisis' have affected each of our monastic communities;[6] when these are the consequence of sinful, false choices that have been made, we recognise that they call for repentance. Especially at such a time, we want to take up the Church's invitation 'courageously to proclaim [our] faith in Christ's death and resurrection that [we] may become a visible sign of this passage from death to life'.[7]

---

[5] Francis, *Address at the Meeting with Seminarians and Novices*, 6 July 2013 (=SN).

[6] VC 63.

[7] VC 63.

4. At the end of the Gospel according to Luke, a book sometimes identified in the tradition as the Gospel of Joy, one story, above all, might speak to our present moment. In chapter 24, Luke recounts the story of Cleopas and an unnamed companion. The two are on their way down from Jerusalem, sad at heart and perplexed, their earlier hopes in Jesus disappointed. Unable to make sense of the reported news of Jesus' resurrection from the dead, they are on their way back home to a village called Emmaus. The present moment for our communities can be felt similarly as one of disappointment and sadness of heart. Many of our houses struggle with numerical decline and fragility of various kinds. Probably all of us are aware of how far we fall short of realising the promises we have made in profession, of the hope we put in the Lord. Like Cleopas and his friend, many of us stand with 'faces downcast' (Lk 24.17). As the Lord comes beside us now as we walk along the road, how is he opening our eyes and ears to see and understand?

5. For this is the point in their 'sad situation of crisis' when Cleopas and his companion encounter 'the Word of God, a Word who calls, who invites, who personally summons'.[8] When Christ re-ignites the joy of his forlorn friends at Emmaus, he extends to them again that originating call, 'the

[8] John Paul II, *Orientale Lumen* (=OL), 10.

joy of the moment in which Jesus looked at me', through a renewed engagement with the Word of God, and through his manifestation of himself within their fellowship at table in the breaking of bread. In the joy of those encounters, they rediscover their commission from the Lord to set out and to tell the story of Jesus, risen from the dead.

6. In the Emmaus narrative, the stranger on the road causes the hearts of the friends to 'burn within them' as he explains to them the scriptures they thought they knew so well, inviting them in effect to revisit their own vocation story. In this Year of Consecrated Life, Pope Francis invites each monk and nun to undertake 'a pilgrimage in reverse';[9] he asks us to re-engage with that originating call of the Lord Jesus out of which our monastic consecration was born: 'to re-read our own personal story and to scrutinise it in the light of God's loving gaze, because if a vocation is always his initiative, it is up to us freely to accept the divine-human economy as a relationship of life in love (*agape*), the path of discipleship'.[10] This statement invites monks and nuns of the English Benedictine Congregation to make a similar pilgrimage, looking back to the essential motives of our own monastic journey as consecrated persons, seeking to identify the beginnings of that journey in

---

[9] CICLSAL, *Rejoice: A Message from the Teachings of Pope Francis* (= *Rejoice*), 4.

[10] *Rejoice* 5.

the word which Christ speaks personally to each of us, and so to receive a deepened theological understanding of our common monastic profession as a fruit of our baptismal participation in Christ's Paschal Mystery.

7. Like the Emmaus disciples, communities of monks and nuns are invited to sit at table with the Risen Jesus, and to 'recognise him at the breaking of bread'. The fraternal communion (*koinonia*) into which our personal encounter with Christ the Word has summoned us, 'is the place where the daily and patient passage from *me* to *us* takes place, from my commitment to a commitment entrusted to the community, from seeking *my things* to seeking *the things of Christ*'.[11] In the face of what Pope Francis has called sterile individualism and identified as the fruit of disheartened fragmentation,[12] monks and nuns 'are invited to humanize community relationships, to encourage communion of heart and spirit in the Gospel sense, because there is a communion of life among all those who belong to Christ'.[13] In this Statement, guided by 'the good zeal which monks and nuns must foster with fervent love' (RB 72), we acknowledge 'the need to promote a spirituality of com-

---

[11] CICLSAL, *Fraternal Love in Community: 'Congregavit nos in unum Christi amor'* (=FLC), 39.

[12] Francis, General Audience, 30 October 2013, cited in *Rejoice* 9.

[13] *Rejoice* 9.

munion, making it the guiding principle' of our praying and living together, of the initial and continuing monastic formation offered within our monasteries, and of the relationships which exist between the houses of our English Benedictine Congregation.[14]

8. At the end of St Luke's account of the Emmaus experience, we read that 'they set out that instant, and returned to Jerusalem'. The commission received from the risen Lord, who at that point made himself known to his disciples, is that the disciples should bear witness to his resurrection by telling the story of how 'they had recognised Jesus in the breaking of bread'. 'The disciple, founded in this way upon the rock of God's word, feels driven to bring the Good News of salvation to his brothers and sisters. Discipleship and mission are like the two sides of a single coin: when the disciple is in love with Christ, he cannot stop proclaiming to the world that only in him do we find salvation'.[15] Monks and nuns recognise that, in common with every baptized person, we receive from Christ the commission to 'preach the Gospel to the whole creation' (Mk 16.15). By our consecration in monastic profession, monks and nuns enter more deeply into this baptismal

[14] John Paul II, *Novo Millennio Ineunte* (=NMI), 43.
[15] Benedict XVI, *Address to the Inaugural Session of the Conference of Bishops of Latin America and the Caribbean*, Aparecida, 13 May 2007 (=AA), 3.

commission, and within the fraternal communion (*koinonia*) of the monastery, which is the fruit of that consecration, we bear witness to a life in which his Gospel is explicitly proclaimed and we prefer nothing whatever to Christ. 'The more consecrated persons allow themselves to be conformed to Christ, the more Christ is made present and active in the world for the salvation of all. Thus it can be said that consecrated persons are *in mission* by virtue of their very consecration, to which they bear witness in accordance with the ideal of their Institute'.[16]

9. This English Benedictine Statement of our monastic and missionary identity is the outcome of a series of theological consultations and discussions established by the General Chapter of 2009. The perspective of the authors has been that 'the life of a Benedictine monk [and nun] requires a continual return, under the impulse of the Holy Spirit and the guidance of the Church, to the Gospel, which is the source and chief guide of all Christian life, and also to the original inspiration of monastic life, which is summed up in the Rule of St Benedict'.[17] The Statement seeks to offer a framework for reflection and for renewal in evangelical and monastic fervour for each monastery of our Congregation, and at the same time is offered to each individual

---

[16] VC 72.

[17] *Constitutions of the Monks of the English Benedictine Congregation*, Declaration 3; cf. Vatican II, *Perfectae Caritatis* (=PC), 2; RB 73.

monk and nun towards the same end. It seeks to stand as a common reference point for the thirteen independent monasteries of our Congregation as they work together to manifest fraternal communion in Christ with one another through shared projects and through mutual support. Finally, the Statement seeks to offer a substantial theological foundation to the work of those tasked with the promotion of the English Benedictine monastic vocation, both in our independent Houses and across the Congregation as a whole.

10. It is with the hope and prayer that 'the sublimity of the knowledge of Christ Jesus' (Phil 3.8) may more fully form us all as monastic men and women of the Gospel 'in power and in the Holy Spirit and with great effect' (1 Thess 1.5) that this Congregational Statement is offered by its authors to the monks and nuns of the English Benedictine Congregation, in this Year of Consecrated Life.

Dom Mark Barrett
Dom Andrew Berry
Dom Alexander Bevan
Dom David Foster
Dame Laurentia Johns

Feast of St Benedict, Patron of Europe, 11 July 2015

CHAPTER ONE

Monastic CONSECRATION in the English Congregation

> The Consecrated Life, deeply rooted in the example and teaching of Christ the Lord, is a gift of God the Father to his Church through the Holy Spirit. By the profession of the evangelical counsels the characteristic features of Jesus—the chaste, poor and obedient one—are made constantly 'visible' in the midst of the world and the eyes of the faithful are directed towards the mystery of the Kingdom of God already at work in history, even as it awaits its full realization in heaven.[1]

11. In its essence, monastic life is an encounter with Jesus Christ. 'The starting point for the monk is the Word of God, a Word who calls, who invites, who personally summons, as happened to the Apostles'.[2] In response to this encounter, monks and nuns join the Emmaus disciples in crying out, 'Did not our hearts burn within us as he talked to us

---

[1] VC 1.
[2] OL 10.

on the road and explained the scriptures to us?' (Lk 24.32). Contemplating the mystery of the incarnate Word, monks and nuns are called to follow his way of life; by profession we undertake to manifest his life by practising the evangelical counsels. By our fidelity to this consecration in monastic profession we are conformed to Christ and come to offer an icon of Christ in the world today.

12. Monastic life makes manifest in the Church that pattern of holiness to which Jesus calls all the baptized. 'In effect, the consecrated life is at the very heart of the Church as a decisive element for her mission, since it manifests the inner nature of the Christian calling and the striving of the whole Church as Bride towards union with her one Spouse'.[3] The effective living out of baptismal identity in consecrated monastic life spells out the eschatological hope of the whole Christian community, for 'it has constantly been taught that the consecrated life is a foreshadowing of the future Kingdom. The Second Vatican Council proposes this teaching anew when it states that consecration better foretells the resurrected state and the glory of the heavenly Kingdom'.[4]

---

[3] VC 3.
[4] VC 26.

The Word who calls

13. In the opening words of the Rule, the monk or nun hears a voice speaking to them, personally and directly. 'Listen carefully, my son, to the Master's instructions, and attend to them with the ear of your heart' (RB Prol.1). The voice in which the divine call is initially heard by a monk or nun may be that of anyone who has mediated to us a sense of Jesus' summons to life. It is not made clear in the text of the Rule precisely who is speaking in the first words of the Prologue. In a similar way, Cleopas and his companion in Luke 24 do not at first know who their fellow traveller is, even when he speaks to them about their deepest concerns.

14. In practice, we find ourselves drawn towards the monastic life by the voices of many who have helped us to begin to listen. The call of Christ is always mediated to us through others: thus, as monks and nuns we are invited to listen and to attend with the ear of the heart to Christ who is always present to us in his Word, especially as the Word listened to and assimilated in the celebration of the liturgy, as well as in the community, in the guest and in the sick.

Encounter and journey with Jesus

15. Throughout our monastic life, as at its start, we continue to listen to Jesus Christ, who has called us. It is by

genuinely listening to his call that we begin to recognise Jesus, the one whom we have encountered. We have sometimes described this encounter as an inner call. With the Gospel as our guide, Jesus shows us that he is himself the path that we must follow in order to come before his heavenly Father. 'The path pointed out by God for this quest and for this love is his Word itself, who in the books of the Sacred Scriptures, offers himself abundantly, for the reflection of men and women'.[5]

16. The Rule dramatizes our encounter with Jesus in the image of the Lord seeking his workman in a multitude of people (RB Prol.14). In this brief image are communicated both the divine initiative, which is the ground of the possibility of vocation, and the universal human quest for life and the desire to see good days that motivates the religious search. For monks and nuns, the relationship between these two perspectives makes the monastery what the Rule calls the *dominici schola servitii* (RB Prol.45). It is within this *schola* that our initial encounter with the Lord is translated into a daily journeying beside him in the company of our brothers and sisters.

17. In some cases, our encounter with Jesus is sudden and life-changing; in others it is the beginning of a slowly germinating seed. Yet in all these situations, we recognise an

---

[5] Plenary CICLSAL.

experience that lies at the heart of the Gospel: 'Being a Christian is not the result of an ethical choice or a lofty idea, but the encounter with an event, a person, which gives life a new horizon and a decisive direction'.[6]

Encountering Jesus in monastic community

18. In the Emmaus story, the encounter with the Risen Jesus at once propels Cleopas and his companion into a restored and deepened communion with the nascent apostolic community in Jerusalem, where they tell their own story, and are confirmed in their faith that 'The Lord has indeed risen' (Lk 24.34). In a similar fashion, the monk and nun discover within their community that communion and fellowship, which enables them to remain 'faithful to the teaching of the apostles, to the brotherhood, to the breaking of bread and to the prayers' (Acts 2.42). The model of the apostolic community in Jerusalem has been seen throughout monastic history as an ideal towards which each concrete monastic community should seek to grow: 'The whole group of believers was united heart and soul' (Acts 4.32). A monastic spirituality is a spirituality of communion. Jesus is himself the source of this unity and communion. He himself promises to be wherever two or three are gathered together in his name (Matt 18.20).

[6] Benedict XVI, *Deus Caritas Est* (=DC), 1.

19. Such a spirituality of communion will be explored in more detail in chapter 2. It is clearly present in the Rule and is expressed most explicitly in chapter 72, on good zeal. The Rule itself uses several images to express the community nature of monastic life. Chapter 1 speaks of cenobitic life in terms of the battle-line where we stand side by side fighting for the true King (RB 1.2; cf. v. 5; Prol.3). In the chapter on the tools of good works, the text refers to the workshop where we persevere (RB 4.78), which picks up the term used in the Prologue for 'school' (v. 45: the Latin word is not exclusively educational as in the modern sense of school). In the main body of the Rule, the most frequent term is *congregatio*, which takes up the image of the flock. The Rule uses the latter term especially in close connection with the care the Abbot owes it as its shepherd.

Spiritual paternity

20. The Rule implies that Jesus' call is personal; it arises through a person's contact with a community, and the life of the community becomes the place where we search for God. It is also the place where Jesus comes to meet us in that search. The Rule prompts us to think of Jesus inviting us into the community, showing us the way of life and, by our attentive listening to the Gospel, we are enabled to follow in his path (Prol.19, 20, 21). In this sense Jesus is the

father, *abba*, of the community, and the Abbot or Abbess is called by that name because the superior is believed to play the part of Christ in the monastery (RB 2.2). This experience of being 'fathered' into adopted sonship in Christ is an experience of the Holy Spirit who creates the communion of the monastic community and empowers its mission (v. 3). In being thus 'fathered' we are drawn into the fullness of divine Trinitarian life.

21. The Abbot or Abbess is often called the 'father' or 'mother' of the community. But the Rule, which never uses this title directly of the superior, says that the head of the household, *paterfamilias*, is God (RB 2.7). The superior is regarded as such in so far as he or she enables members of a community to grow in this sense of being beloved children of their heavenly Father. The Rule does not discuss the complementary gender roles of 'mothering' or 'fathering'; its concern is to promote the personal lives of each monk or nun in relationships of fraternal and chaste love (cf. RB 72.8). A superior's discernment should accordingly seek to promote the life of the Spirit within the community and the fullest sharing of his gifts to each of its members.[7]

---

[7] Monastic communities need to "promote a generative, not simply administrative, dynamic to embrace the spiritual events present in our communities and in the world, movements and grace that the Spirit works in each individual person. We are invited to commit ourselves to dismantling lifeless models, to describing the human

22. The Rule is clear that the Abbot's or Abbess's place in the community must be understood within a context of faith (*creditur*, RB 2.2). More recently, the exercise of authority by a superior in the Church has been explained in terms of their encouragement of growth of fraternity within such relationships of communion. The Latin word for authority, *auctoritas*, is derived from the verb *augeo-ere*, to cause to grow, as in to augment. The Rule itself reserves this word for Scripture and the Rule (RB 9.8; 37.1; 73.3). For these are the source of life and growth in the monastery, since all authority comes from God (Rom 13.1). Monastic superiors are themselves under authority (RB 63.2-3; cf. Lk 7.8) but have power to act and to make decisions (RB 39.6, *arbitrium et potestas*). We understand how the Abbot or Abbess holds the *place* of Christ in the monastery in this light. More precisely, the Rule uses the phrase *vices Christi agere*. Since the Rule draws a neat distinction between status and service (*praeesse* and *prodesse*, RB 64.8), the old translation of *occupying a place* is probably less helpful than that of *playing a role* or doing a job, imitating the Lord who came to serve and not be served (Matt 20.28; cf. Phil 2.5-11). This is the paradoxical foundation of the Abbot's or Abbess's *dignitas* (RB 2.1). RB 2 also talks about the Abbot's or Abbess's leadership in terms of their role of teaching (RB 2.1, 11),

---

person as marked by Christ, who is never revealed absolutely in speech or actions" (*Rejoice* 12).

amplified later in the Rule by other roles, all of them associated with socially inferior positions: shepherd (2.8, 9, 39; 27.8), doctor (27.1; 28.2) and steward (*vilicus* cf. 64.7). We can see too how the language of command (*imperia*, RB 64.17) is offset by that of burden and fragility, mercy, forethought and consideration (*onus*, v. 7; *fragilitas*, v. 13; *misericordia*, v. 9, 10; *providentia, consideratio*, v. 17). In their service of the brethren, the Abbot or Abbess helps us listen to the Father by seeking to continue Jesus' service of his disciples at the Last Supper as a ministry of communion.

23. The Rule assigns entirely to the superior (*maior*) the care for a community's structures of authority and administration, for example, by the Prior and other officials. The spiritual qualifications needed by them suggest too how spiritual paternity is dispersed through the leadership of the community. Deans need to live a holy life and be able, like the abbot, to teach (RB 21.1, 4). The cellarer, in particular, is 'like a father' (RB 31.2); he and the Prior should fear God; there are *senpectae* (RB 27) and spiritual fathers mentioned apart from the abbot (RB 46.5; 49.9) while all the seniors should be regarded with fatherly reverence (*paterna reverentia*, RB 63.12). But the point of paternity is fraternity. When referring to individual monks or nuns, the term *frater* (brother) is frequently used. This spells out what should be a characteristic relationship between members of the community. It is the term generally used in the

early church, together with its feminine form, for the community of the baptized. The Rule never uses the word for family. Although its provisions suggest a family style of relationship, the monastery has to be seen as a supernatural faith community, and not reduced to human terms of 'togetherness'. The spiritual paternity of the Abbot and Abbess not only refers to their mediation of the Trinitarian experience of being born again in the Spirit (cf. Jn 3.3-16); it is also something that, thanks to their ministry, is dispersed throughout the human relationships of fraternity.

Formation and growth to our full stature in Christ

24. Monastic life should both be a call to a deepening encounter with Christ in the community and also help us grow to our full stature in Christ (Eph. 4.13). The Rule teaches that in doing so we come to share in the Paschal mystery of Jesus' own path through suffering to glory (RB Prol.49-50). The workshop of the monastery is the place where our practice of the spiritual craft prepares us for the unspeakable joys of heaven (RB 4.75-78). Although we ascend there by the ladder of humility, with its clear allusions to Christ's passion (RB 7.34, 35-36), our perseverance in monastic life is also seen as a work of grace in the development of a Christ-like character through the transformation of our nature. By growing in the experience of Christ's love, fear should be cast out, so that we come to

Monastic Consecration in the English Congregation 21

the love of God. It is no doubt timely that the Rule encourages us neither to be daunted by nor to run away from what may be asked of us, but it is good when individual monks and nuns can share their experience that this is a way of growing that brings delight and expands our hearts to more generous love (Prol.48-49). Ours is a life where we should find our natural gifts acknowledged, encouraged and put to good use (cf. *bonis suis in nobis*, Prol.6); it is also a life where, through prayer, grace works with nature in surprising ways, to transform us in ways that often cannot be foreseen (cf. *et quod minus in nos habet natura possibile*, Prol.40-41).

25. Monks and nuns are pilgrims together on their community's path of discipleship: 'Religious community is not simply a collection of Christians in search of personal perfection [. . .] it is a living expression and privileged fulfilment of its own particular *communion*, of the great Trinitarian *koinonia*'.[8] The first seeds of Christian life were sown for us in baptism-confirmation; while there are monks and nuns appointed to assist a novice or junior in the early stages of monastic life, monastic formation is a life-long process, where everyone needs each other to deepen their lives of faith, hope and love and to grow to their full stature of life in Christ. 'In the entire dynamic of

[8] FLC 2.

community life, Christ, in his paschal mystery, remains the model of how to construct unity. Indeed, he is the source, the model and the measure of the command of mutual love: we must love one another as he loved us. And he loved us to the point of giving up his life for us. Our life is a sharing in the charity of Christ, in his love for the Father and for his brothers and sisters, a love forgetful of self'.[9]

26. Formation is fundamentally God's work through the Holy Spirit, who 'shapes the hearts of [us] all' (Ps 32) and who never takes his hands from the clay.[10] Each of us is personally responsible for co-operating with the one who is 'powerful enough to reform what in us is deformed'.[11] We need each other's support too, as example, help and friend. This is why the Rule exhorts monks and nuns to the good zeal of mutual obedience (RB 71–72).

27. This transforming collaboration works gradually through the practice of monastic life (*conversatio morum*). This is the principal medium for continuing, or on-going, formation, with the various channels that contribute to it. The liturgy, attentive listening to the Word of God, prolonged in silent personal prayer, is perhaps the primary

---

[9] FLC 21.
[10] Cf. Irenaeus, *Adversus Haereses* V.1.3.
[11] Augustine, *Confessions* IX.6.14.

means; the formal preaching and teaching in the community, personal study and reading by a monk and nun, as well as the enrichment of cultural experience, for example, in arts and music, are precious ways of growing in wisdom and experience of the ways of God. No less important can be the experience of the natural world and social relationships. All can help us open our hearts more generously to God, who also comes close to us in the lives of those we meet or serve.

Monastic profession

28. The initiative in monastic life is God's (Jn 15.16). He calls and we respond to his call. The response we learn to make is the gift of our whole selves, as an acknowledgement of all God has given us. Even giving our whole lives is not done simply on our initiative; our desire and capacity for it is tested and trained, it has to be recognised by the community in whose company we seek God. The promise we make in giving ourselves wholly to God's service is invited, received and affirmed by the community in the name of the whole Church. All this is included in monastic profession. It contributes to making monastic profession a consecrated form of life in the Church. The Church blesses and God makes holy.

29. Monastic profession is expressed in a promise made by a monk or nun (RB 58.17). The promise is nowadays

initially for a limited period, and finally for the whole of their life. It is a threefold promise of a person's stability, *conversatio morum* and obedience. It is embodied in a written petition (RB 58.20), which is received by the superior, signed and placed by the candidate on the altar where it is associated with the offering of the Mass. This unites the candidate's self-gift to that of the whole community, which offers itself to God in union with Jesus' own gift of himself to the Father's glory for the salvation of the world.

30. The Rule includes a corresponding ritual whereby a monk or nun removes the clothes of ordinary life and is clothed by the superior in the religious habit. It marks a renunciation of one form of life in favour of another, not to condemn ordinary life, but to state a decision to seek the Kingdom of God before all things (cf. RB 58.26-28). The monastic habit symbolizes the clothes of a human nature made new.[12] They are what we need for the steep and narrow path by which we seek to find the treasure of our heart (RB Prol.48; Matt 7.14; 6.19-21; 13.44-46). The newly clothed prostrate themselves at the feet of the brethren, seeking their prayers, and at the same time being raised up by them in a fraternal sign of peace and love in recognition that we

---

[12] "May the Lord clothe you with the new nature, created in the likeness of God, in righteousness and holiness". Norms for the rite of admission into the novitiate 7, *The Monastic Ritual of the English Benedictine Congregation*, 1994 (2007).

are one body in Christ, a community united in his service (RB 58.23).

31. In the English Congregation, as elsewhere in the Benedictine world, these rituals have been restructured to cover the whole period of initial monastic formation. The key point is that clothing and profession are integrally part of a single formation process, one that speaks of the central reality manifested in a person's vowed consecration to monastic life.

32. The profession of monastic life commits monks and nuns to the values of the Gospel and to a life that seeks to make the Kingdom of God a reality in this world. As a solemn and public act, recognised and blessed by the Church, the profession of their vows strengthens a monk's or nun's human capacity for fidelity to God within their community.

Evangelical counsels, evangelical lives

33. The promise we make in monastic profession is of our stability, our *conversatio morum* and obedience. While not formally mentioning the evangelical counsels of poverty, celibate chastity and obedience, by monastic profession we undertake the evangelical life those counsels express. Although they became the conventional formula for religious profession after the Rule, the Rule already points in

their direction when it observes that monks and nuns cannot claim anything as a private possession (poverty) because they have already renounced possession of their own bodies (celibacy) and wills (obedience) (RB 33.4).

34. By stability, we undertake to persevere in the monastic way of life that we have discovered in the fraternity of a particular community and its practice of fidelity to Jesus Christ. The rootedness of a particular community's life is not primarily about geographical location. It includes its history, and the wisdom it has inherited; the rock is Christ (1 Cor 10.4).

35. Our *conversatio morum* refers to the life-style and practices that express the wisdom of the monastic tradition that underlies and has shaped the houses of our Congregation. This way of life is how *this* community has encountered Christ and has become the path that we believe is marked out for us so that we can find God.

36. Obedience is in the first instance obedience to God and to his will, which we believe is disclosed for us in the community and in its obedience to his word. As such we believe that the Abbot and Abbess, by their decisions and teaching, help us to grow in that obedience, which we live out in serving the good of our brethren and of all people committed to our care. This is the blessing, the *bonum*, of mutual obedience that Benedict extols in the Rule (RB 71.1).

37. Vocation and consecration are from start to finish a personal relationship with Jesus. Celibate chastity in particular expresses the fact that Jesus is the one to whom we look for intimacy and in whose humanity and love for all we hope to find the fulfilment of our sexuality and personal identity. The structures of life in a monastery and in the Church are important only to the extent that they sustain human relationships in Jesus, and give them a specific shape and purpose as a way for us to find the fullness of life in bearing witness to him. 'In purgatory there are more monastics who have sinned through blind fidelity to tradition than through being daring in their creativity in order to communicate our monastic tradition. Let those who have ears, hear!'[13]

---

[13] Abbot Bernardo Olivera, OCSO, *Greeting to the Benedictine Abbots' Congress* (Rome, 2004).

CHAPTER TWO

Monastic COMMUNION in the English Congregation

> By constantly promoting fraternal love, also in the form of common life, the consecrated life has shown that sharing in the Trinitarian communion can change human relationships and create a new type of solidarity. In this way it speaks to people both of the beauty of fraternal communion and of the ways which actually lead to it. Consecrated persons live *for* God and *from* God, and precisely for this reason they are able to bear witness to the reconciling power of grace, which overcomes the divisive tendencies present in the human heart and in society.[1]

38. At Emmaus the disciples invited the stranger to supper with them. And when he took the bread, 'their eyes were opened and they recognised' that it was Jesus himself who had been beside them throughout their journey (Lk 24.31). It was a moment of communion even as he vanished from their eyes, which prompted them to return to Jerusalem to

---

[1] VC 41.

bear witness to what had happened. This was a second moment of communion between the Emmaus disciples and the Eleven and those who were with them (vv. 33-35). It symbolizes the ecclesial nature of communion. The culmination of the story is when Jesus comes openly into their fellowship. They feel the fear of God (v. 37) but also joy (v. 41), and Jesus shares his peace with them in the promise of the Spirit (v. 36).

39. This twofold dynamic of human fellowship can be found in a monastic community and in its relations with the whole Church. Jesus discloses himself in moments of communion; in and through such moments he helps us discover our communion with each other. That communion is a call to bear witness together with the rest of the Church to the living presence of the Lord, who comes into our midst with the gift of the Spirit. The mystery of the fullness of life, and his power over death draws us into a living awareness of God's own life as Father, Son and Holy Spirit. The mystery of the Resurrection reveals in this way the Trinitarian mystery, which lies at the heart of Christian communion, which monastic life strives to make a human reality for all to see and share. 'This special way of "following Christ", at the origin of which is always the initiative of the Father, has an essential Christological and pneumatological meaning: it expresses in a particularly vivid way the Trinitarian nature of the Christian life and

it anticipates in a certain way that eschatological fulfilment towards which the whole Church is tending'.[2]

40. The cenobitic character of monastic life has deep theological roots, which Part 1 of this chapter will outline. A monastic community can be thought of as a school of communion that needs to be supported and nourished; Part 2 of the chapter will present the ways in which this God-given mystery of communion is supported and nourished. Formation within the school of communion is discussed in Part 3 under the heading of monastic integrity as an education in love. In particular, the traditional goal of purity of heart has to be related to the development of a positive affectivity. Growth in such integrity is the monastic path of holiness. In Part 4, the role of the English Benedictine Congregation in sustaining and nurturing such a communion between our houses will be considered.

Part 1: A theology of monastic communion

Church and monastery as communion

41. The term communion (*koinonia*) is one of the earliest words used in the New Testament to refer to the Christian community as such (cf. Acts 2.42-47). Paul uses *koinonia* to refer to the mutual reciprocity of life within the Trinity that

[2] VC 14.

is completed by the gift of the Holy Spirit and shared with us (2 Cor 13.13). Christians are called into this *koinonia* through Jesus Christ our Lord (1 Cor 1.9), a life nourished and celebrated above all in the Eucharistic *koinonia* (1 Cor 10.16). Implicit in this conception is the belief that human relationships in the Church and the structures that support them are born within the relationship with him that Jesus makes possible through his Resurrection (cf. Jn 3.5-8).

42. The word *koinonia* means sharing something in common. Pachomian monks used it as a name for their communities in southern Egypt, where monastic life was lived in common (*koinos bios*). It refers to the way monks and nuns tried to see their lives as ecclesial, as manifesting the communion of the Church. In Syria, where monks were known by the Syriac word for Jesus' name, the only-begotten (*ihidaya*), the earliest monastic communities were called 'covenants'. The ideal of *koinonia* was further developed by Augustine of Hippo, who reinforced the picture of communion in the apostolic community, stating that the brethren should 'dwell together in unity in the house and be of one mind and one heart unto God'.[3]

43. It has become a key term in the Church's self-understanding, especially in the thought of John Paul II: 'communion (*koinonia*) which embodies and reveals the

---

[3] *Rule of Augustine* I.2.

very essence of the mystery of the Church [. . .] is the fruit and demonstration of that love which springs from the heart of the Eternal Father and is poured out upon us through the Spirit which Jesus gives us, to make us all one heart and one soul. It is in building this communion of love that the Church appears as "sacrament", as the "sign and instrument of intimate union with God and of the unity of the human race"'.[4]

Monastic communion reflects the life of the holy Trinity in the Church

44. While it is true that 'at times religious communities are fraught with tensions, and risk becoming individualistic and scattered', it is simultaneously the case that 'the humanising power of the Gospel is witnessed in fraternity lived in community and is created through welcome, respect, mutual help, understanding, kindness, forgiveness

---

[4] NMI 42. *Religious and Human Promotion* (1978) (=RHP), 24, speaks of religious as 'experts in communion'. The importance of the theme of communion is developed in *Fraternal Life in Community* (1994), 3, which refers to a change in terminology in the Code of Canon Law (1983) where the idea of common life in a merely external sense is replaced by phrases such as fraternal life and communion. The idea plays a prominent part in *Vita Consecrata* (1995), 46, 50, 51, 72; *Novo Millennio Ineunte*, 43–45; *Starting Afresh from Christ*, 28–29, 30, 32, 34; and *Africae Munus*, 34–35.

and joy'.[5] The fraternal life of the monastic community is 'a God-enlightened space in which to experience the hidden presence of the Risen Lord'.[6] Among the members of such a monastic fraternity, a communion (*koinonia*) of mind and heart can come to be, precisely because a monastery is a human community in which the Trinity dwells. 'It is the Spirit himself who leads the soul to the experience of communion with the Father and with his Son Jesus Christ, a communion which is the source of fraternal life'.[7]

45. The sacramental dimension of communion expresses the strong sense that Jesus makes himself present through the gift of the Holy Spirit in the human relationships that constitute the life of the community. 'A spirituality of communion indicates above all the heart's contemplation of the mystery of the Trinity dwelling in us, and whose light we must also be able to see shining on the face of the brothers and sisters around us. A spirituality of communion also means an ability to think of our brothers and sisters in faith within the profound unity of the Mystical Body, and therefore as "those who are a part of me". This makes us able to share their joys and sufferings, to sense their desires and attend to their needs, to offer them deep and genuine

---

[5] Francis, *Address to Participants in the General Chapter of the Salesian Society of St John Bosco* (=SGC).

[6] VC 42; Basil, *Short Rules*, 225.

[7] VC 42.

friendship'.[8] Luke says it all: 'They were filled with joy and with the Holy Spirit'[9] (Acts 13.52).

46. In this sense, monastic communion is a particular manifestation of the communion of the Church's life and stands as a sign of the mystery of life, both human and divine, to which the whole Church is called. Thus, the lives of monks and nuns are a living parable of what the Body of Christ must be on earth: '[a] Church which "goes forth" [. . .] a community of missionary disciples who take the first step, who are involved and supportive, who bear fruit and rejoice'.[10]

Monastic communion as a fruit of the resurrection of Jesus

47. The resurrection of Jesus brings this reality of communion to birth in the Church. Monastic communion (*koinonia*) is the experience of Easter night, when Jesus met his disciples in the upper room in a moment of welcome, joy and peace, of forgiveness. The encounter was also an experience of the Holy Spirit, whether as promised or as given (Lk 24.49; cf. Jn 20.22). Meeting the risen Jesus is thus marked by the outpouring of new life in the Spirit, and, by means of his healing, empowering and transforming

---

[8] NMI 43.
[9] Cf. FLC 11.
[10] Francis, *Evangelii Gaudium* (=EG), 24.

human relationships, he sends the disciples out to invite all humankind into communion.

48. This communion cannot be kept to ourselves. When the promise of the Spirit was fulfilled at Pentecost, the disciples were all together in one place; their communion was empowered to speak so that all could hear the voice of God (Acts 2.1-6). Communion and mission are always profoundly interconnected.[11] Mission is a source of renewal. Otherwise there is a risk that a community falls victim to a kind of ecclesial introversion.[12] 'It is in building this communion of love that the Church appears as sacrament, as the sign and instrument of intimate union with God and of the unity of the human race'.[13]

Monastic communion and sharing in the self-emptying of Christ

49. We find the fullness of life as Christ did, by giving it away for the sake of the Church, his body, and for the good of all for whom he gave his life. St Paul thinks of this process as a kenosis, or 'self-emptying' (Phil 2.6-11). 'Did not the Christ have to suffer these things and so to enter into his glory?' (Lk 24.26).

---

[11] Cf. John Paul II, *Christifideles Laici* (=CL), 32.
[12] Cf. John Paul II, *Ecclesia in Oceania* (=EO), 19.
[13] NMI 42.

50. Monastic communion (*koinonia*) is not to be taken for granted; it has to be achieved by the tools of good works (cf. esp. RB 4.22-26) and continually renewed by the Lord's prayer for forgiveness, 'because thorns of contention are likely to spring up' (RB 13.12). The Rule speaks of the patience by which we share in the passion of Christ (Prol.50), a patience that includes mutual obedience, taking the initiative in working for reconciliation (RB 72.6; 71.6-9), the good zeal of letting others come first in our thinking and a generous bearing of the physical and personal infirmities of the brethren (RB 72.5, 7).

51. The last discourses in John's Gospel, chapters 13–17, are a sustained reflection on this process, one of building communities that share Jesus' friendship (cf. Jn 15.15). Monastic communion flourishes in friendship where we are able to follow the Lord's example: where we wash the feet of others as we seek to make welcome, where we always seek for reconciliation, and where we place ourselves at each other's service. Through such choices, 'rather than living in some utopia, you will find ways to create "alternate [*sic*] spaces", where the Gospel approach of self-giving, fraternity, embracing differences, and love of one another can thrive'.[14]

---

[14] Francis, *Apostolic Letter to All Consecrated People on the Occasion of the Year of Consecrated Life* (=YCL), II.2.

Part 2: A school of communion

52. *Communion* is the standard translation of *koinonia*. Its Latin root is linked to the idea of mutual exchange. The Rule speaks of communion only for Holy Communion; it uses *fraternitas* to refer to the human community; but, as we have already noted, fraternal relations in a monastery are brought about by our engagement with the exchanges of life that flow from responding to the divine initiative of call and consecration. The school of the Lord's service is where monks and nuns learn and practise communion. Life according to the Rule gives a daily experience of it, and provides for its support and nourishment. This is how monks and nuns are able to grow in communion to the wholeness of monastic integrity that is traditionally called purity of heart.

The daily experience of monastic communion

53. Strong moments in the life of a community, such as professions, ordinations and abbatial blessings, are so because they express monastic communion. Monastic communion is particularly apparent at the funeral of a monk or nun, where a community celebrates the conclusion of a monastic life; such occasions testify to how a monk or nun has striven to give their life away in obedience to Jesus' example of love to the end. Along the way, even in trials and setbacks, a community gives thanks for God's presence

in the life they have shared, and how through God's grace communion has been strengthened.

54. Communion is also experienced in the ordinary round of daily work, whether manual and repetitive, professionally burdensome or intellectually demanding. This is what the Rule refers to as living by the work of our hands (RB 48.8; cf. 2 Thess 3.10-12). The necessity of earning our living gives a community practical ways of sharing things as simply as possible, of together taking up the cross of Christ each day to follow him and bear good fruit for eternal life. The underlying dignity of this reality can be seen when a community gathers for prayer, arriving at different paces and with their different abilities and disabilities, 'each of us disabled or wounded in some way yet together for better or worse, included and not to be lived without'.[15] It is how our monasteries can be places where the Kingdom won for us by Christ breaks in.

55. Monastic communion (*koinonia*) involves cultivating an ethos where monks and nuns are valued as human beings with something to contribute at every stage of their life.[16] As Pope Francis has taught, 'Disregard for the duty to cultivate and maintain a proper relationship with my neighbour, for whose care and custody I am responsible, ruins

---

[15] An EBC monk.
[16] Cf. VC 70.

my relationship with my own self, with others, with God and with the earth. When all these relationships are neglected, when justice no longer dwells in the land, the Bible tells us that life itself is endangered'.[17] The communion of the monastery is in this way to be counter-cultural in an age where earning power and the instrumental capacity to produce increasingly hold sway.

56. On the journey, as the Rule makes very apparent, particular concern must be shown for the needs of the sick, elderly, young and those who are frail and vulnerable in other ways: those on the margins, those in danger of being consumed by work, the disillusioned and wayward (RB 2; 27; 36; 58; 64; 72). The concern here is for brothers and sisters in need, a concern to be shared by every monk and nun in the monastery where we are called to bear each other's burdens (Gal 6.2; cf. RB 72.5). 'All of this, however, is not in the nature of the "old man", who wants communion and unity but does not want or intend to pay the price in terms of personal commitment and dedication. The path that leads from the "old man", who tends to close in on himself, to the "new man" who gives himself to others is a long and difficult one'.[18]

---

[17] Francis, *Laudato Sì* (=LS), 70.
[18] FLC 21.

57. As 'homes and schools of communion [. . .] a spirituality of communion means, finally, to know how to "make room" for our brothers and sisters [. . .] and resisting the selfish temptations which constantly beset us and provoke competition, careerism, distrust and jealousy. Let us have no illusions: unless we follow this spiritual path, external structures of communion will serve very little purpose. They would become mechanisms without a soul, "masks" of communion rather than its means of expression and growth'.[19]

Supporting monastic communion

58. Monastic communion (*koinonia*) is supported by the complementary roles of Abbot or Abbess, Rule and community. The leadership of the Abbot or Abbess is part of their role in engendering a monastic response to Jesus, but as such it needs to be considered together with other elements supporting communion. These include the methods for consultation, discernment and decision-making in the community.

LEADERSHIP IN PROMOTING MONASTIC COMMUNION

59. Chapter 1 has already outlined the various images used in the Rule to describe abbatial leadership in the community,

---

[19] NMI 43.

and the complex way in which the relationship of a monk or a nun to the superior is one where the leadership in a community exists to promote fraternity and mutual responsibility, not dependence.

60. We have noted too how others collaborate in abbatial leadership, both administratively and spiritually. There are other officials of the monastery too, responsible for formation and the care of the infirm and the elderly. The superior's responsibility for hospitality is also delegated. Some of these roles have formal responsibilities within the whole community, others are more occasional and concern the care exercised by the Abbot or Abbess for individual brethren. The task of all these officials is to foster the communion of the monastery. All are appointed by the Abbot or Abbess and contribute to their overall leadership so that they can confidently share their burdens (cf. RB 21.3). The vertical dimension of authority, of leadership and obedience, should promote the horizontal dimension of community relationships and mission to those outside the monastery.

61. We can speak of a charism of presence, watching, supporting, encouraging, challenging, stretching, consoling, as well as correcting; it is also a work of prayer and love. It demands a long-term and costly investment of energy. While the Rule assumes that the service of the Abbot or Abbess entails a commitment for the rest of their life, this

has been practised in various ways, including fixed terms with re-election, which has been the practice in the EBC, or unlimited terms of office subject to review at Visitation. An important principle for the Rule is that other officials, who are all appointed by the Abbot or Abbess, thereby collaborate in the mission of leadership that ultimately belongs to the superior.

CONSULTATION, DECISION, DISCERNMENT

62. The Rule allocates a separate chapter for 'calling the brethren for counsel' (RB 3). In doing so Benedict differs from the Rule of the Master, which subsumes the community aspect into the chapter on the Abbot or Abbess. The Rule of St Benedict embodies a spirituality of communion where everyone has a voice, including the youngest members. In asserting this, the Rule envisages that the community is continually trying to listen to what the Holy Spirit is saying to it (cf. RB Prol.11-12). The monastic Chapter and Council should be seen as a way of listening to the voice of the Lord and of responding to his will.

63. The Rule makes clear that the principle of discernment should be the Rule itself (RB 3.7). The Rule is the criterion for listening to what God is saying to a community, as the Rule points out, often in its youngest members (RB 3.3). It is the Abbot's or Abbess's responsibility to listen to all and to decide; the superior is to hold to the teaching of

God's word, and decide in the fear of God and in accordance with the Rule. To do this, all monks and nuns need to be well informed of the matters in hand, as well as of developments in the day-to-day life of the community. Obedience grows out of a deep sense of listening, of appreciation and of common discernment of what God is working to achieve in and through the community.

64. There are biblical models for such a collaborative approach to the exercise of authority; but in its deepest sense it reflects our Trinitarian faith in a community of persons each fully attentive to the others in the work of redemption.

MONASTIC ENCLOSURE

65. In the Egyptian desert, the boundary walls of a monastery would be the most obvious thing about a monastery from the outside. But within is an oasis. Such walls define and protect a distinctive environment, and the Rule too is concerned that a monk leaves it at his peril (RB 66.7). The monastic enclosure, which fosters a monastic life of prayer, affords the environment where a community is able to grow in the stability of its *conversatio morum*.[20] It is also a sign of the interior life, a symbol of the enclosure of the heart where God has chosen to dwell. Enclosure does not

[20] Cf. PC 9.

mean keeping others out—guests bring a special grace and should never be wanting in a monastery; for the Rule, enclosure is more about keeping monks in, for the good of their souls. That does not mean that they don't go out, even according to the Rule; but they go out with a purpose—not just on their own initiative just to wander around (RB 67) or for private social purposes which would diminish communion (RB 51.1).

66. Enclosure plays a particular part in the life of the nuns of our Congregation, but for all our houses enclosure makes monastic life a prophetic sign, helping it raise a question about the values of a culture in which freedom of movement is regarded as a blessing by many but where homelessness and globalisation is also experienced by many more as a curse. Our monks have been allowed to serve overriding pastoral needs of the Church outside the enclosure, but this should not compromise a monk's growing closer and closer to God (cf. RB 62.3-4).

67. Monastic community speaks very physically of God's presence in the world, as well as showing how the world finds its ultimate meaning in what lies beyond. That is a further reason for the value given to the architecture of a monastic church and buildings. Beauty raises human hearts and minds to the divine. It is not only a matter of aesthetic experience. Monastic buildings speak the language of transcendence, pointing beyond themselves as

potent signs of the primacy of the spiritual and of lives consecrated to God.

Nourishing monastic communion

68. Communion is founded on Christ's presence in a monastic community, and his gift to it of the Holy Spirit. The depth of communion in a community is expressed and sustained in terms of its human relationships, but it is nourished by its spiritual life.

EUCHARIST AND LITURGY OF THE HOURS

69. The communion of a monastery, as is that of the Church as a whole, is a sacramental reality; it is nourished sacramentally, above all, by the Eucharist, where the Risen Jesus himself makes himself really present in the midst of his followers. In each of our communities the solemn celebration of the Mass is the summit and source of the monastery's life. The drama of Christ's life from death animates the rhythm of that life in all its times and seasons. Flowing from this, and leading the community into it, the regular celebration of the Liturgy of the Hours occupies a primary place in the day. The Rule understands this, rather than any other activity, as the work of God (*Opus Dei*); according to the Rule, nothing should be preferred to this worship which consecrates the day to the glory of God, and leads the monk and nun, awakened to a sense of God's presence

in all things and all people, to a life of continual prayer. Like Moses, we seek to enter into the tent of God's presence where he can speak to us as a man speaks to his friend (Ex 33.11).

LECTIO DIVINA AND PERSONAL PRAYER

70. Benedictine life is centred on prayer. It is how we listen to Jesus calling us, and how we meet him in his living word. Scripture, 'truest of guides for human life' (RB 73.3), is a privileged place of encounter with Jesus. Listening communally to God speaking to us in the Scriptures, we are drawn more deeply into communion with one another and with the whole Church. The Word is both source and sign of unity. It purifies the heart (Jn 15.3; 1 Pet 1.22) and frees us to be drawn into the mutually indwelling relationship promised by the Word, and fits us to be true disciples and friends (Jn 8.31; 15.7, 14).

71. In *lectio divina* we appropriate in a personal way the Scriptures heard in the liturgy so that they open up the depths of our heart in prayer and contemplation. This vital contact with the Risen Christ is transformative. Both the faithful practice of *lectio divina* and a substantial period of time devoted each day exclusively to personal prayer help a monk or nun to engage with the mystery of Christ at the deepest level of their personal lives. 'Every day the monk is nourished by the bread of the Word. Deprived of it, he

is as though dead with nothing left to communicate to his brothers and sisters because the Word is Christ to whom the monk is called to be conformed'.[21]

72. While *lectio divina* is normally practised in personal reflective prayer, it may also be shared. The Manquehue Apostolic Movement, with which our Congregation shares close bonds, has helped our monasteries, schools and parishes begin to discover the ways in which *lectio divina* strengthens communion in a friendship with Jesus that flows out in mission.

PRAYING AT ALL TIMES; PRAYING FOR ALL PEOPLE

73. Within their pursuit of continual prayer, monks and nuns try to look at the world with a 'spiritual gaze born of deep faith which acknowledges what God is doing in the lives of others',[22] bearing the needs of all mankind in their heart in prayer that God's kingdom come and his will be done. They seek to share the world's hunger for bread and its thirst for life; to suffer with others' need for forgiveness and for perseverance in their struggle for good over evil. The ministry of intercessory prayer, offered both publicly and personally, flows out as part of the monastic mission in solidarity with the joys, hopes, griefs and anxieties of

---

[21] OL 10.
[22] EG 282.

this age. 'When evangelizers rise from prayer, their hearts are more open; freed of self-absorption, they are desirous of doing good and sharing their lives with others'.[23]

A CONTEMPLATIVE LIFE IN COMMUNION

74. '[Intercession] does not divert us from true contemplation, since authentic contemplation always has a place for others. [. . .] Intercession is like a "leaven" in the heart of the Trinity. It is a way of penetrating the Father's heart and discovering new dimensions, which can shed light on concrete situations and change them'.[24]

75. In our Congregation, there has been a particular tradition of teaching contemplative prayer, which is witnessed to by the English mystics, and which was given authoritative recognition in the Congregation by Augustine Baker's *Holy Wisdom*. His teaching unites the contemplative tradition of the English mystics, with an interpretation of the traditional goal of monastic life as union with God attained under grace by means of asceticism and prayer.[25]

76. This teaching was a source of strength in the seventeenth century, as in the monastic renewal of the late nineteenth century; it is still relevant for monks and nuns in

---

[23] EG 282.
[24] EG 281; 283.
[25] Cf. Cassian, *Conferences* I.

the struggle to train their thoughts so as to receive the Spirit's gift of contemplative prayer in purity of heart. By it, they strive to grow in the 'love that impels them to pursue everlasting life' (RB 5.10). At the same time contemplative prayer is enriched by the liturgy and *lectio divina*, which in turn are enriched by contemplative prayer.

Part 3: Monastic integrity and communion

77. In order to be a school of communion, a monastery has to be a school of love. Only so can it be a place for human growth and flourishing.[26] In its proper sense, communion (*koinonia*) is a gift of God, making himself present in the midst of Jesus' disciples as a love that draws them together even when there is little or nothing at a natural level to unite them. Fraternal life in communion is about how a community's way of life (*conversatio*) expresses and realises that fullness of life which Jesus, the template of true humanity, shares with the Church.[27]

78. This is not automatically brought about by the Rule and customs of a monastery, though they are intended to promote it. It is realised in the good zeal of monks, in the

---

[26] FLC 25; 35. The expression is from William of St Thierry's *Caritatis Schola: De natura et dignitate amoris* IX, 26; cf. Bernard, *De Diversis* 121.

[27] Cf. *Redemptor Hominis*, 8; *Gaudium et Spes*, 22.

cultivation of the life of virtue which breaks with faults and leads to God; it calls for a fervent love shown in mutual encouragement and support, seeking the good of others; a chaste love born of a sense of the spiritual bonds that unite the community (cf. RB 72).

79. While the habits of selfishness and sin remain the same, in every generation and for everyone, communities have to address particular challenges together. They are a call to repentance, to deeper faith and conversion of life, and also to renew the hope that has inspired our brethren, who are for us examples of the true humanity and holiness we recognise in Jesus. With our eyes fixed on him, they are signs of the joy that lies before us (cf. Heb 12.2).

80. Contemporary appreciation of the affective dimension of human life, of the need for psychological balance and emotional maturity in order to live a healthy monastic life, goes beyond the text of the Rule, but it does not lie beyond its perspective. The Rule speaks of the need to love God with the whole heart, soul and strength, and to love one's neighbour as oneself (RB 4.1-2). The tools of good works discussed by the Rule teach those who practise the spiritual craft the length, breadth, height and depth of that love (Eph 3.7). It is the perfection of love, which casts out fear (RB 7.67), the newness of life that requires monks to die to sin by the faithful practice of humility. It requires the purification of hearts by the Holy Spirit (RB 7.70), learning to live

in the full truth of our own frailty, as well as that of God's unfailing loving kindness.

81. Every Christian reality is founded on frailty,[28] which is why growth in monastic communion depends on collaborating with the grace and transforming work of the Holy Spirit. Psychological insights as well as more traditional monastic wisdom teach how to grow in self-knowledge and mutual understanding, how to seek forgiveness and work for reconciliation. This wisdom helps monks and nuns grow in emotional depth and affective maturity, 'which is a pre-requisite of a radiant evangelical life';[29] it is characterized by their readiness to let the primacy of Jesus' love be the law of new life that sets them free to give themselves to others in the spirit of his friendship.

82. The Prologue envisages that a community will need to address monastic failure but that it should also promote charity (RB Prol.47). The recurrent challenge of 'doing one's own thing', 'going one's own way' (*propria voluntas*) that leads to a more stubborn self-will (RB Prol.3; 3.8; 4.60; 5.7; 7.12, 19; 33.3-4; cf. the sarabaites, 1.11) can be converted into the joyful spontaneity of living in hope of Easter (RB 49.6-8). The discipline of the Rule is consequently explicitly directed against occasions where pride surfaces in mur-

[28] FLC 25; 35.
[29] FLC 28; cf. 37.

muring, opposition to monastic living and contempt of the brethren (cf. RB 23.1).

83. Thanks to its purifying work, the Spirit opens the human heart more fully to God in prayer (RB 20.1, 3, 4), in a developing union, which is expressed in monastic life by the communion of fraternal life and which is attained by that means.

84. Purity of heart bears a richer fruit in promoting a monastic culture of peace-making and reconciliation as a further witness to divine mercy in the world (RB Prol.17; 4.29, 73; 34.5). In the face of the serious conflicts and violence around us, the example of communities striving to live together despite differences and difficulties is a sign of how God can transform human lives and relationships to be signs of his own power to make all things new in the Kingdom. Fraternal communion is a prophetic sign of how God is at work in the particular human lives of a community. As a prophetic sign it points ahead to a reality that is already at work in the fellowship of those who are striving for that Kingdom. 'Fraternal love in Christ changes human relationships and leads to a new solidarity'.[30]

85. The evangelical counsels that lie at the heart of consecrated life testify to this. They show the positive meaning

---

[30] VC 41.

of monastic asceticism. They express our faith and hope that the fullness of life is realised in the image of Jesus' humanity. He shows that they are not an impoverishment of truly human life but its liberation and transformation by the Holy Spirit. God is the absolute good, and our overriding love. Celibate chastity for the Kingdom of heaven is not a denial of sexuality but a choice to dedicate our capacity and need for love to relationships and friendship that make manifest Jesus' pure and undivided love of the Father.[31] Evangelical poverty does not deny the value of material things but affirms that true wealth is found in calling nothing our own and in ordering material life by the values of the Kingdom of heaven.[32] Dedicating ourselves to obedience expresses our faith that perfect freedom is found in God's will.[33]

86. The evangelical counsels express a faith that human life can speak the language of God's love. They speak of a new attitude to the whole created order, which the Rule hints at in the reverence it suggests is due to the ordinary implements of working life (RB 31.10). This instinct in Benedictine life has been articulated strongly in Pope Francis's encyclical, *Laudato Sì*, in calling for an integral ecology on the basis of God's revealing himself in every element of

[31] VC 14; 16; 18; with a special reference to celibacy, 88.
[32] VC 89.
[33] VC 91.

his creation.[34] As stewards of God's gifts, we are accountable to God and to succeeding generations for the legacy we have received. A sense of solidarity with, and commitment to, the poor should as a result inform our use of the earth's resources and should be reflected in a lifestyle which is simple and frugal in keeping with the spirit of poverty demanded by the Gospel and our Rule.

Part 4: Communion and solidarity in the EBC

87. Monastic communion is an expression of ecclesial communion,[35] a charism whose authenticity is marked by ecclesiality.[36] The uniqueness of each vocation and the particular vocation of any community means that no two paths are exactly the same. Within the Church's mission our monasteries have a common history from which they draw inspiration and encouragement, not least from the example of the pastors and martyrs during times of persecution and the many faithful witnesses that have inspired monks and nuns across the ages. Together, we traverse terrain charted by a monastic, Benedictine and English Benedictine tradition in the footsteps of a 'great crowd of

---

[34] LS esp. 137–55.
[35] FLC 10.
[36] EG 130.

witnesses' who have preceded us who inspire us (cf. Heb 12.1-2).

88. Monastic congregations have been established among other purposes to promote renewal, support and reform in individual houses. The English Benedictine Congregation likewise in our day is considering how best to support individual monasteries in their fidelity to Jesus' invitation to the fullness of life.

89. The Congregation has also encouraged the development of a number of collaborative processes to promote initial and ongoing formation. While our communities are aware of the difficulty of providing effective teaching and of stimulating the quality of learning that monastic life needs, the Congregation is trying to develop ways of co-ordinating available resources. Meetings of novices and juniors in our monasteries have been valued as ways of bringing young vocations into contact with each other at an early stage of monastic life. They have helped foster communion within the Congregation.

CHAPTER THREE

Monastic COMMISSION in the English Congregation

> In the image of Jesus, the beloved Son 'whom the Father consecrated and sent into the world' (Jn 10.36), those whom God calls to follow him are also consecrated and sent into the world to imitate his example and to continue his mission. Fundamentally, this is true of every disciple. In a special way, however, it is true of those who, in the manner that characterizes the consecrated life, are called to follow Christ more closely, and to make him the all of their lives. The task of devoting themselves wholly to *mission* is therefore included in their call; indeed, by the action of the Holy Spirit who is at the origin of every vocation and charism, *consecrated life itself is a mission*, as was the whole of Jesus' life.[1]

90. The fraternal communion (*koinonia*) of a monastery is also generative for the wider Church and for the world through *mission*, which by its nature extends beyond the monastery. As Pope John Paul II has taught, 'Religious life

---

[1] VC 72.

[. . .] continues the mission of Christ with another feature specifically its own: *fraternal life in community for the sake of the mission*.[2] It is not something that can be kept safely secure to a small group; as a gift of the Spirit it is integrated into the body of the Church. This is a sure sign of the authenticity of a charism.[3] Religious life needs to be lived energetically and reinterpreted culturally. It is not distilled water, but yeast![4]

91. In the Emmaus story, the transformative moment 'at the breaking of bread' when Cleopas and his companion recognise Jesus, 'and their eyes were opened', is at one and the same time an experience of fiery joy and an event which propels them to 'set out that instant', with the intention of telling their story 'of what had happened on the road and how they had recognised him at the breaking of bread'. It is in this moment of recognition that the disciples return to the apostles in Jerusalem. They realise their communion with the whole Church, in which Jesus makes himself present and commissions them; fraternal communion becomes a sending out in communion, a com-mission. 'Go, therefore, make disciples of all nations' (Matt 28.19).

---

[2] VC 72.

[3] Cf. EG 130.

[4] Cf. Antonio Spadaro, 'Wake Up the World: Conversation with Pope Francis about Religious Life', *Civiltà Cattolica* 165, no. 1 (2014).

92. For the monk or nun, 'the task of devoting themselves wholly to mission'[5] is the same thing as their consecration in monastic profession and the sharing of their lives in monastic communion (*koinonia*). Just as in monastic consecration 'the characteristic features of Jesus [. . .] are made constantly "visible" in the midst of the world',[6] in the fraternal communion of monastic life 'the experience of the complete sharing with Christ lived out by the Twelve'[7] is made really present in human society. Thus, to say that, for monks and nuns, 'consecrated life itself is a mission' is to affirm that the mission of monastic life 'consists in making Christ present to the world'.[8]

93. This is how Benedictine monks and nuns can be seen as responding to the Church's 'greatest need in the present historical moment', since they will be 'people who make God credible in this world by means of the enlightened faith they live [. . .] who keep their eyes fixed on God, learning from him what true humanity means. We need people whose intellect is enlightened by the light of God,

---

[5] VC 72.
[6] VC 1.
[7] VC 41.
[8] VC 72.

[people] whose hearts are opened by God, so that their intellect can speak to the intellect of others and their hearts can open the hearts of others'.[9]

94. English Benedictine monks and nuns recognise with evangelical joy that we are commissioned within the Church to make Christ present in the world; as individual monks and nuns, through a profound and personal dedication to the Lord Jesus in our monastic consecration; as monastic communities, through a fraternal communion of life (*koinonia*) lived out in our monasteries; and through the ardent dedication of each of our monasteries to the specific mission it has received in the local church and to its continuing development as a living witness to the Gospel.[10]

Monastic consecration for the sake of mission

95. Chapter 1 of this Statement examined in some detail the implications for monks and nuns in the English Congregation of our consecrated lives within the Church. Here, we must make Pope John Paul II's affirmation our own. 'The first missionary duty of consecrated persons is to themselves, and they fulfil it by opening their hearts to the

---

[9] J Ratzinger, *Christianity and the Crisis of Cultures*, 52–53.
[10] Cf. VC 72.

promptings of the Spirit of Christ. [. . .] Consecrated persons will be missionaries above all by continually deepening their awareness of having been called and chosen by God, to whom they must therefore direct and offer everything that they are and have, freeing themselves from the obstacles which could hinder the totality of their response'.[11]

96. The Rule asks of each monk and nun who begins to follow a monastic life that we truly seek God, and that we show eagerness for the Work of God, for obedience and for trials (RB 58.7). It is precisely this profound and personal dedication to Jesus Christ brought by faithfully living out the Rule, the 'law under which you are choosing to serve' (RB 58.10), which will constitute our engagement with this first missionary duty. 'The fact that consecrated persons fix their gaze on the Lord's countenance does not diminish their commitment on behalf of humanity; on the contrary, it strengthens this commitment, enabling it to have an impact on history, in order to free history from all that disfigures it'.[12]

97. For the Rule, monastic identity is founded on a response to the injunction to 'open our eyes to the light that comes from God, and our ears to the voice from heaven that every

[11] VC 25.
[12] VC 75.

day calls out' (RB Prol.9). Writing of monastic life, Pope John Paul II notes, 'When a person is touched by the Word obedience is born, that is, the listening which changes life'.[13] Monastic holiness is the fruit of this obedience, the fruit of this openness to the action of God's word in the lives of individual monks and nuns, who thereby offer a missionary witness both within and beyond the monastery. 'The specific contribution of consecrated persons, both men and women, to evangelization is first of all the witness of a life given totally to God and to their brothers and sisters, in imitation of the Saviour who, out of love for humanity, made himself a servant'.[14]

98. The origins and history of our Congregation reinforce this theological insight. Gregory the Great and the monk-missioner Augustine of Canterbury recognised the value of monastic communities as centres for the evangelisation of Saxon England, where monks and nuns were able by the integrity of their lives in community to sow the seeds of faith in the local culture and nourish its growth. Their monasteries also bore fruit in the evangelisation and nurturing of Christian culture on the European continent. Thus it was natural that Gregory and Augustine should inspire

---

[13] OL 10.
[14] VC 76.

the renewed vision of our Congregation in the seventeenth as well as in the late nineteenth centuries.

99. Martyrdom has been a part of that tradition, above all, in the seventeenth century, with which the pastoral mission of our Congregation has been closely linked. The passion of the martyrs for Jesus prepared them to give their lives for others. It is important for our generation to recover the deep value of this tradition to inspire us in the present context. For this it is a help to recover the links between red martyrdom and the 'white martyrdom' of renunciation in monastic life. In the martyr monks the radical cost of witnessing to Jesus, and the wholeheartedness of response to him, shows the seriousness, integrity and authenticity of monastic life. The earliest monastic literature sees martyrdom in the conflict any monk or nun must endure with the demons of the desert in the struggle for purity of heart and the perfect love of God. The challenge of selflessness in promoting a true *koinonia* bears witness to the perfect love of Jesus who made himself obedient unto death. Similarly the glory of the martyrs lies in what they lived for rather than their death; their lives show what ultimately counted.

100. As a complete giving of life, martyrdom is a way of expressing how religious consecration overflows in evangelical joy. Pope Francis teaches that the missionary effectiveness of consecrated life 'depends on the eloquence

of your lives, lives which radiate the joy and beauty of living the Gospel and following Christ to the full'.[15] The Rule uses the same idea at the end of the Prologue 'as we progress in this way of life and in faith, we shall run on the path of God's commandments, our hearts overflowing with the inexpressible delight of love' (RB Prol.49). It has to be shared with others.

Monastic communion for the sake of mission

101. In Chapter 2 the monastery was thought of as the school of communion that the Risen Jesus shares with his disciples. This is a further sense in which our monastic life contributes to the mission of the Church that *goes forth*: 'an evangelizing community knows that the Lord has taken the initiative, he has loved us first, and therefore we can move forward, boldly take the initiative, go out'.[16] In particular the Church calls monks and nuns to be 'experts of communion'.[17] This is how we are able 'to live the present with passion'.[18] Pope John Paul II also taught that 'the sense of ecclesial communion, developing into a spirituality of communion [. . .] becomes a sign for all the world and a

---

[15] YCL II.1.
[16] EG 24.
[17] RHP 24; FLC 10.
[18] YCL I.2.

compelling force that leads people to faith in Christ. [. . .] In this way communion leads to mission, and itself becomes mission'.[19]

102. There is a dynamic inherent in monastic community that, while it draws its members more closely together in communion, animates them at the same time to 'go forth' in missionary joy. John speaks of it in the image of the vine when Jesus tells the disciples to remain united in his love (Jn 15.9-10), and in his gift of peace (Jn 14.27), but where they also find the joy (Jn 15.11) that drives them in love to go out and bear fruit (Jn 15.16). Mutual love (Jn 15.18) leads to testimony (Jn 15.27). 'Go forth', like the idea of mission, is measured more by how far we *live* communion out than of how far we *go* out. It means making Christ present in the world.

103. There are a number of biblical images and models that help make strong connections between these two dimensions of our life. Gregory's *Dialogues* refer to Benedict as a light set on a lampstand: 'like a shining lamp his example was to be set on a lampstand to give light to everyone in God's house' (cf. Matt 5.15).[20] He also describes Monte Cassino as a town on a high mountain, the top of which

---

[19] VC 46; cf. CL 32.
[20] Gregory the Great, *Dialogues* II.1.

touches the heavens;[21] this invites us to think of the biblical imagery of a city on a hilltop, like Jerusalem, where the Temple stands, from which water flows to give life to a new creation, and which in the fullness of time will have no walls but where everyone may find access. Pope Benedict XVI notes that, after his formation in the solitude of Subiaco, he made his foundation at Monte Cassino, the 'city on the hill' where, in the midst of the ruins of pagan culture, he evangelized the local people and there 'assembled the forces from which a new world was formed'.[22] He taught that 'Monastic life has its *raison d'etre* in withdrawal and concealment, but a monastery also has a public role in the life of the Church and of society'.[23]

104. In a different field of imagery, Gregory refers to the parables of the sower, describing Benedict's life as welltilled soil and cleared of briars (*ibid.*, 3) that is able to bring forth a rich harvest. The Gospels talk of the fruitfulness of a tree (Matt 7.16-18), where holiness of life is itself lifegiving and welcoming (Matt 13.31). The image of salt (Matt 5.14) and yeast (Matt 13.33) can be a way of seeing how our lives really only find their sense within a broader context, giving flavour or helping to transform the lives of others.

[21] *Ibid.*, 8.
[22] *Christianity and the Crisis of Cultures*, 52–53.
[23] Benedict XVI, General Audience, 9 April 2008.

Mission and the work of the monastery

105. Monastic work flows out of our life for others. We discover the evangelical gift of new life in giving our lives away, sharing them with others like Christ. Monastic communion (*koinonia*) is shared in the space where we make room for others; it is the fruit of kenosis in the way we are able and willing to kneel at the feet of others in order to make them welcome at the table of the Lord.

106. Our constitutions on monastic work reflect this insight in starting from the evangelical motive of Christian discipleship. 'Our monks are engaged principally in the work of spreading the gospel, through parish work that has been traditional in our Congregation since the seventeenth century, through educational work, and through studies. (*Religiosus Ordo*) Our Congregation should nevertheless look forward to adapting the work that has distinguished it in the past to the needs of the present and of the future'.[24] The *Apostolatus Benedictinorum in Anglia* (1626), which was grounded on the work of Augustine Baker and Leander Jones, noted at the very beginning of the story of our Congregation that the four charisms of the Congregation were the solemn celebration of the liturgy, hospitality, enclosure and study. We need to re-appropriate the grace God has

---

[24] EBC Constitutions, Declaration 45.

given us in our tradition in order to bear richer fruit for the future.

107. Our brethren have spoken both of the joy and privilege of being able to share in this mission, especially in parochial and pastoral work, and of the way in which it has helped them grow to a sense of the fullness of life that draws us on the monastic path to Christ. But they have expressed concern about the need to keep the necessary balances within the common life and also in their personal life so that they can persevere in responding to the Lord's continual call to follow him, rather than find themselves trapped in demands that become a source of conflict. Imbalance and overwork is one kind of problem. It is also easy to forget the value of study. The pressures of external demands, as well as the stimulus of working with other people, tend to crowd out the time and energy available for monastic study and scholarship, as well as for other forms of intellectual creativity. Our Congregation has made distinguished contributions in these fields in the past, and the monastic tradition of matching a love of learning with the desire for God can be a precious contribution to the renovation of Christian culture.[25] They are in any case an important part of a healthy monastic life.

---

[25] Cf. VC 98.

108. In our monasteries of nuns, too, the disappearance of the categories of lay and extern sister, but not of their tasks, has been a new challenge to the need to balance work, prayer and *lectio divina* as well as study. It has added considerable demands on some who have to do the extra work, which has meant a major rethink is called for. While the response to these demands is often generous, the necessary psychological adjustment, for example, in accepting the new situation can take longer and be a cause of tension.

109. The Rule is aware of this concern for the harmonisation of the demands of daily monastic life, and specifically of the problem that work can marginalise *lectio divina* and become an obstacle to the prayer needed for monastic life to flourish (RB 48). The opening verse, 'idleness is the enemy of the soul', is more famous than the chapter itself, which does not give the priority to work, but is concerned to safeguard and prioritise *lectio*. It is aware of the danger of half-heartedness and of the needs of those who get bored by having too much time on their own (RB 48.23). So idleness can be a problem, and work a solution. Overwork is not a problem the Rule addresses, except in relation to the exceptional circumstances of the harvest (RB 48.7); however, it is clear that the sick and less sturdy souls need to be given appropriate work, which is a principle that can be generalised (RB 48.24-25). A monk or nun needs to be candid with their superior if the practical burdens make the personal dimension of monastic life impossible (RB

68); the superior has to take responsibility for making a just judgement about the spiritual good (cf. RB 2.33-34; 3.11).

110. These are matters of concern for all and need to be addressed with creativity and personal honesty to promote a healthy re-integration of work with the rest of monastic life. However, the needed balance and moderation have nothing to do with mediocrity. On the contrary, the Rule calls us to live the radical spirit of the Gospel with all that implies for love of God, love of neighbour and self. From deep listening, in poverty of spirit, to the various demands made on us comes the grace of discretion; we learn to ask for our needs in prayer, as well as how to prioritize and when to ask for, or to offer, help (see RB 31.17; 53.18-20).

111. While the conscience of each monk and nun is sacrosanct, personal responsibility in fraternal life means we are accountable to each other for our use of time and resources. If monastic consecration means that our bodies and wills are no longer at our own disposal, by the same token the community must be concerned for individual well-being. A lack of concern for individuals affects the community and undermines communion.

Monastic hospitality as a means of evangelisation

112. The gates and thresholds of a monastery are places where Jesus can be welcomed in the guise of a stranger

(RB 53.1). In recent years our monasteries have all discovered a renewed appreciation of hospitality as a means by which they can share the communion that animates their lives; the various ways in which this has been done should be seen as forms of evangelisation. They include ways of opening up the traditional hospitality to retreat groups, to forms of catechetical and adult education in faith and to guidance in Christian vocation. As a sign of ecclesial communion, we are glad to make our monasteries available to others as places for spiritual refreshment. In some cases we know that contact with a monastic community is able to offer people an experience of the Church that they cannot otherwise access. Hospitality can be experienced through personal contact as a call to conversion, to renewal of life and to growth in an understanding of faith and vocation. Hospitality makes it possible to reach out to those who feel alienated from the Church. It has been a way in which the priestly ministry of reconciliation has been exercised. This kind of work has inspired some telling images like open cloister, compass points and stepping-stones; they complement more traditional ones like sanctuary and oasis.

113. For a monastic community, authentic living of the Gospel can make an innovative contribution to meeting the challenges of inculturation; as it engages with the culture and issues of our own societies it can find effective ways of inculturating the mystery of faith and of evangelising

the culture. 'As a sign of the primacy of God and his Kingdom, it can, through dialogue, elicit a positive reaction in people's consciences. If the consecrated life maintains its prophetic impact, it serves as a Gospel leaven within a culture, purifying and perfecting it'.[26]

114. Pope John Paul II called for an evangelisation that is new in fervour, new in methods and new in its expression.[27] Our monasteries must seek to respond by being 'continually open to challenge by the revealed word and the signs of the times'.[28] This calls for monasteries as well as individual monks and nuns to be thoroughly evangelized themselves, and able to discern the theological significance of the challenges of our time. Above all it means being attentive to the ways in which a relatively prosperous society has lost its religious and spiritual orientations, where the sense of human being and culture has been depleted as a result. It also means being attentive to the ways in which people are excluded from a just share in the economic prosperity or political participation in our society.[29] Pope Francis teaches that the Church is evangelised by the

---

[26] VC 79.

[27] John Paul II, *Address at the Opening of the 19th Ordinary Plenary Assembly of the Latin American Episcopal Council*, 9 March 1983 (=CELAM III).

[28] VC 81.

[29] Cf. VC 82.

poor, just as God became poor to enrich us by his poverty (2 Cor 8.9).[30] We must not forget the attention the Rule gives to the poor in renewing our understanding of hospitality (RB 31.9; 53.15).

The monastery within the local church

115. The specific ways in which we have tried to share the charism of our monastic life beyond the confines of the community need to be understood closely in connection with the part it plays in the life of the wider Church. The genuine communion of a monastic community can be found only in relation to the Church as a whole, and especially to the local church.[31]

116. Lay oblates are a particular way in which a monastic community is able to share the fraternal communion of its life with lay people who seek to leaven the dough of their ordinary lives and their service of the mission of the local church with the yeast of Benedictine wisdom. They have responded to a call, been through a process of discernment and formation and have made a promise to witness to Benedictine life in their homes, at work and in the local church. The part that oblates play in the individual communities where they make their oblation varies, but the

---

[30] EG 197–99, quoting Benedict XVI, AA 3.
[31] Cf. CRSI, *Mutuae Relationes* (1978).

Pastoral mission and English Benedictine monasticism

117. Whether as monks or nuns, we are conscious of having inherited a tradition of participation in the pastoral mission of the local church. In the seventeenth century it was seen in terms of external missionary work in the extreme circumstances of persecution and penalties faced by ordinary Catholics who wanted to practise their faith. It was an exceptional undertaking. From the beginning, the overriding needs of those who were deprived of sacraments and pastoral care were recognised by our brethren who risked their lives to serve as priests in England and Wales. As part of this work our nuns continued to support the mission by their contemplative life of prayer.

118. Subsequently the 'mission' came to refer to the parish work that developed from this. It was undertaken around the country, often in areas of poverty and social hardship. These were conditions in which one could speak of martyrs of charity. The martyrs that had been a strong thread in our Congregation's sense of identity could still be relevant to the sense felt in missionary life that the call to radical discipleship is one 'costing not less than everything'.

119. But a community's evangelisation does not only happen away from the monastery; all the more strongly can it be furthered around the monastery itself, where the community as a whole is able to contribute to it through its fraternal life in communion. This has been a characteristic feature of the development of our life in the twentieth century, in local parishes and centres in and near the monastery, as well as in what has been described in connection to hospitality.

120. Our monasteries all have close ties to other Christian churches. The fact that our community life is rooted in baptism and religious profession, and not defined only by the sacraments that have divided Christian communities, means that we can be places where ecumenism can be promoted in a particular way. Monastic communities can make a particular contribution to ecumenical dialogue, especially through *lectio divina* and prayer, including the Liturgy of the Hours.[32] These are strong elements in monastic life where other Christians can be generously included.

121. Many of our houses have ties to other faith groups, where our lives of prayer and our witness to the sanctity of natural signs encourage a spirit of dialogue. Above all, monks and nuns are able to share the genuine humanity

---

[32] VC 101.

that flourishes in a life of poverty, chastity and humility, and which can promote dialogue of faith and a common concern for compassion and justice, as well as care for the sick and needy. Our monks and nuns have noted that their communities can bear particular witness in our time through their reverence for human life and a due appreciation of the environment when the earth's resources are in jeopardy.[33]

Educational mission and English Benedictine monasticism

122. The educational mission of the English Benedictines is currently lived out in adult education, in universities, in the secondary and primary schools associated with our monasteries or served by them and in a number of innovative and less formal settings. This specifically monastic mission finds its place within the wider mission of the Catholic Church in education, whose centre and foundation is the person of the Lord Jesus, and his command to share the Good News. 'Founded on the mandate received from Christ, [the Church] seeks to cast light on cultural values and expressions, to correct and purify them, where necessary, in the light of faith, in order to bring them to

---

[33] VC 102.

their fullness of meaning'.[34] Our mission in the world of education is among the ways in which the fruits of monastic learning become available to nourish the hearts and minds of those among whom we minister and to further their human maturity and sense of their vocation. Within this educational mission, the Benedictine school has occupied a special place.

123. Benedictine schools, like all Catholic schools, exist 'to be part of the Church's mission, to place Christ and the teaching of the Catholic Church at the centre of people's lives'.[35] Pope Benedict XVI has spoken of education as 'integral to the mission of the Church to proclaim the Good News. First and foremost every Catholic educational institution is a place to encounter the living God who in Jesus Christ reveals his transforming love and truth'.[36] In addition, our schools play a part in the mission of the wider Church, as 'means of helping parents to fulfil their role in education',[37] and to this end they provide an especially high quality of partnership with families and of religious education. Finally, our schools play a part in the life of their

---

[34] Congregation for Catholic Education, *Presence of the Church in University* (=PCU) II.1.

[35] Marcus Stock, *Christ at the Centre: Why the Catholic Church Provides Catholic Schools* (=CAC 1).

[36] Benedict XVI, *Meeting with Catholic Educators* (=MCE).

[37] Code of Canon Law, 796.1.

local dioceses and of the localities in which they are situated, thereby seeking to be 'a public good whose benefits enhance the whole community'.[38]

124. A Benedictine school, rooted in the mission of a monastic community, is established to be a 'school of the mind of the Son',[39] within which it is possible 'to promote a spirituality of communion capable of becoming the educational principle' by which the school both *educates* and *forms* young people.[40] In this regard, the Benedictine school enjoys a unique relationship with its founding Benedictine monastery, for 'the consecrated life can be compared in some ways to a school', and monks seek to share within their schools not only what they themselves have come to know of 'the mind of the Son' but especially the manner by which they have come to know it.[41]

125. Thus, in the context of a Benedictine school, to *educate* is to 'help young people to grasp their own identity and to reveal those authentic needs and desires that inhabit everyone's heart, but which often remain unknown and underestimated'.[42] Benedictine education is explicitly

[38] CAC 4.

[39] Congregation for Catholic Education, *Consecrated Persons and Their Mission in Schools* (=CPMS), 11.

[40] CPMS 15.

[41] CPMS 9.

[42] CPMS 18.

founded in a clear articulation of values drawn from the Gospel and mediated by the living out of the Rule: our students will 'thirst for authenticity and honesty, for love and fidelity, for truth and consistency, for happiness and fullness of life. Desires which in the final analysis converge in the supreme human desire: to *see the face of God*'.[43] Catholic teachers, both monastic and lay, have a vital role to play in this task.

126. A Benedictine school *forms* young people when it explicitly recognises the need to mentor, to offer role models, and to accompany its students as they seek to understand themselves and to discover their God-given vocation in life through the education they are offered. The witness and ministry of monks, themselves formed in the monastic 'school of the mind of Christ', who work as teachers and as chaplains in our schools is of crucial importance in this regard. Their lives 'propose that form of existence which is inspired by Christ, so that even a young person may live the freedom of being a child of God'.[44] Benedictine monks thereby bring to bear upon their schools a perspective that is genuinely prophetic in the contemporary educational landscape.

---

[43] CPMS 18.
[44] CPMS 19.

127. Benedictine schools today are to be understood as primary contexts of the New Evangelisation. With the Church as a whole, monks and nuns can see that 'particularly in countries with ancient Christian roots [. . .] entire groups of the baptized have lost a living sense of the faith, or even no longer consider themselves members of the Church, and live a life far removed from Christ and his Gospel'.[45] Among those whose lives are touched by our Benedictine schools, some can be recognised as falling within this description, and it may be that their number is growing. It is already the case that for some families, and many young people, schools such as ours constitute their only real point of contact with the Church. Our schools are therefore called to an evangelisation 'new in its ardour, methods and expression',[46] understanding themselves to be among those 'wells where thirsting men and women are invited to encounter Jesus' and actively seeking 'to offer oases in the deserts of life' where this encounter may become a lived daily reality.[47] Thus, our schools should seek to offer a 'creative apologetics'[48] through their curriculum and a consistent ethic of Christian life through their every-

---

[45] John Paul II, *Redemptoris Missio* (=RM) 33.

[46] CELAM III.

[47] Synod of Bishops, *Message from XIII Ordinary General Assembly*, 2012.

[48] EG 132.

day participation in the fraternal communion (*koinonia*) of monastic living.

128. Benedictine schools are rooted in the consecrated life and fraternal communion of the particular monastery by which they are each commissioned to live and work as a 'school of the mind of the Son'.[49] While today monks sometimes work alongside lay school governors, leaders, teachers and ancillary staff, it is now usually the case that the pivotal roles within Benedictine schools are entrusted to lay people: 'it is the lay teachers, and indeed all lay persons, believers or not, who will substantially determine whether or not a school realizes its aims and accomplishes its objectives'.[50] The further development by the English Benedictine Congregation, and by the individual monasteries, of programmes of formation for all of our professional lay collaborators in the Catholic ethos and Benedictine identity of our schools, along with a fuller articulation of and training in their educational philosophy, is a significant area of monastic endeavour; 'it is an indispensable human formation, and without it, it would be foolish to undertake any educational work'.[51] In such an endeavour an active role

[49] CPMS 11.
[50] Congregation for Catholic Education, *Lay Catholics in Schools* (=LCS), 1.
[51] LCS 16.

can be played by all houses of the Congregation, not only by those who directly sponsor a particular school.

Source and summit of monastic life

129. The gift of fraternal life in communion of the monastic community finds its proper expression in the celebration of the liturgy, the source and summit of all Christian life, 'for the aim and object of apostolic works is that all who are made sons of God by faith and baptism should come together to praise God in the midst of his Church, to take part in the sacrifice and to eat the Lord's supper'.[52] In the same way, after the disciples from Emmaus told the disciples all that had happened, Jesus himself came into their presence, to renew his gift of peace and joy, and to share the disciples' food with them, the fish, which soon became a symbol of the Church's faith and life (Lk 24.36-43).

130. The *Opus Dei*, an expression which the Rule reserves for the liturgical prayer of the monastic community, is the work of God in the double sense of what we do for God, as well as what God does for, in and through us. For this reason the Church commissions a monastic community to celebrate the Eucharist and the Liturgy of the Hours in

---

[52] Vatican II, *Sacrosanctum Concilium* (=SC), 10.

full.[53] For in the liturgy we proclaim the name of the Lord until he comes again. We do so by celebrating the Lord's mighty works in salvation, the mystery of reconciliation and new life. We also stand in prayer giving voice to the whole of creation as it acknowledges its creator and hope.[54]

131. Sharing in the celebration of the liturgy is a source and fruit of communion,[55] which our constitutions state 'has a particular value in building up the unity of the monastic family in communion and in manifesting Christ and the Church to the world'.[56] By it, the work of our redemption is accomplished, the Church is built up and, as we are built into a holy temple to the Lord,[57] the earthly city trains its eyes in expectation of the heavenly Jerusalem.[58] The liturgy teaches us to read our lives and the world around us in the context of our celebrating God's mighty works and his repeated call to his people to 'go forth'; the Holy Spirit refreshes the memory and deepens our understanding of all that Jesus has said as the word of God who created the heavens and the earth; the same Spirit leads us into the whole truth (Jn 16.4, 8, 13).

[53] SC 95.
[54] Cf. OL 8; 10–12.
[55] PC 15.
[56] EBC Constitutions, Declaration 24.
[57] SC 2.
[58] VC 6.

132. It is an essential means by which a monk or nun deepens and renews the consecration which they initially made in union with the Sacrifice of the Lord; it is an offering which must become a reality in our passion to live out the gift of ourselves to the full.[59]

133. This is what makes the liturgy a central place of evangelisation. Pope Francis notes that it celebrates the task of mission and is the source of renewed self-giving. Not only that, but a liturgy is given its beauty by the joy with which it is celebrated in a community that is invigorated by a sense of its evangelical mission.[60] It is central to the monastic desire to 'live the present with passion' and to 'Wake up the world'.[61]

---

[59] Cf. Paul VI, *Evangelica Testificatio*, 47.
[60] EG 24.
[61] YCL I.2; II.2.

AFTERWORD

To Wake Up the World

134. In calling on religious to 'wake up the world', Pope Francis is calling for prophets. 'The distinctive sign of consecrated life is prophecy. [. . .] This is the priority that is needed right now: to be prophets who witness to how Jesus lived on this earth [. . .] a religious must never abandon prophecy'.[1] This English Benedictine Statement has been written to support the monasteries of our Congregation in their response to this challenge; it seeks to offer the resources of monastic theological reflection as a contribution to this process.

135. To do this, the monasteries of our Congregation are invited to engage in what has been called a conversation, guided by their Abbots or Abbesses. This statement is offered as, so to speak, the first words in such a conversation. It does not try to touch on every aspect of the lives of our monasteries; as the conversation continues other issues will probably become clear that need exploration, as well

---

[1] YCL II.2.

as some mentioned here that need fuller treatment. What this statement has tried to offer is a reading of the monastic reality of our lives and its grounding in the Rule and in the Word of God, in the light of the Church's teaching on religious life, the call to renewal, and the call to evangelisation. In trying to say what it means to be an English Benedictine monk or nun today, its aim is to help us listen to the challenge that Jesus' call holds for each of our communities. It is the challenge to live prophetically.

136. A clear response from monks and nuns to this call to live prophetically does not imply any flight from a proper concern for the world. Pope Benedict XVI points out that the mistake that might be made today, as in past ages, would be to suppose that 'monasteries were places of flight from the world (*contemptus mundi*) and of withdrawal from responsibility for the world, in search of private salvation'.[2] He cites Bernard of Clairvaux, that magnet of monastic vocations, as a leading proponent of a very different view. For Bernard, the monastery was the place where the labours of the few, for whom he uses the term 'contemplatives', dedicated to the taming of the overgrown thickets both of the forest and of the soul, bring life to the many, since, as Pope Benedict observes, 'no positive world order

---

[2] Benedict XVI, *Spe Salvi* (=SS), 15.

can prosper where souls are overgrown'.³ Such a spiritual ecology is the prophetic task that monks and nuns perform for the whole Church and for the world.

137. With Pope John Paul II, we believe that 'the monastery is the prophetic place where creation becomes praise of God and the precept of concretely lived charity becomes the ideal of human coexistence; it is where the human being seeks God without limitation or impediment, becoming a reference point for all people, bearing them in his heart and helping them to seek God'.⁴ For monks and nuns, God's call is total; this is why we have been consecrated in monastic profession and so enter more deeply into our baptismal commission. Within the fraternal communion (*koinonia*) of the monastery, which is the fruit of that consecration, we bear witness through an evangelical life in which Christ's Gospel is explicitly lived out and proclaimed that we 'prefer nothing whatever to Christ'.

138. In conclusion, we recall the words of Pope Francis for the Year of Consecrated Life: 'I want to say one word to you and this word is "joy". Wherever there are consecrated people [. . .] there is joy, there is always joy!'⁵ And

---

³ SS 15.
⁴ OL 9.
⁵ *Rejoice* 12.

alongside these words we place these words of Fr Augustine Baker, written specifically to English Benedictines:

> St Paul exhorts, saying: *Gaudete in Domino semper, iterum dico, Gaudete*; Do you always joy or rejoice in our Lord; I say again, rejoice ye. Good Lord, how much & how often, both in the Epistles of St Paul & in other places of the Holy Scripture, but especially in the New Testament, we are encouraged & exhorted to this joy! For it is joy that we aim at even in this life; & the mean, the more it partaketh of the end, the better it is, & charity, joy, & peace are numbered to be the prime fruits of the Holy Ghost; & how many texts are there in the Scripture against inordinate sadness, & experience & reason do shew the harm of it.[6]

---

[6] Augustine Baker, *A Spiritual Treatise Entitled Confession*, pp. 119–21, c. 1628.

REFERENCES USED IN THE STATEMENT

DOCUMENTS OF VATICAN II

Gaudium et Spes. Pastoral Constitution on the Church in the Modern World (1965).

Perfectae Caritatis. Decree on the Adaptation and Renewal of Religious Life (1965). (=PC)

Sacrosanctum Concilium. Constitution on the Sacred Liturgy (1963). (=SC)

PAPAL DOCUMENTS

Paul VI. *Evangelica Testificatio*. Apostolic Exhortation on the Renewal of the Religious Life according to the Teaching of the Second Vatican Council (1971).

John Paul II. *Address at the Opening of the 19th Ordinary Plenary Assembly of the Latin American Episcopal Council* [CELAM], III, Port-au-Prince Cathedral, Haiti, 9 March 1983; *L'Osservatore Romano*, English edition (18 April 1983), 9. (=CELAM III)

———. *Christifideles Laici*. Post-synodal Apostolic Exhortation on the Vocation of the Lay Faithful in the Church and in the World (1998). (=CL)

———. Code of Canon Law (1983).

———. *Ecclesia in Oceania*. Post-synodal Apostolic Exhortation on Jesus Christ and the Peoples of Oceania: Walking His Way, Telling His Truth, Living His Life (2001).

———. *Novo Millennio Ineunte*. Apostolic Letter at the Close of the Great Jubilee of the Year 2000 (2001). (=NMI)

———. *Orientale Lumen*. Apostolic Letter to Mark the Centenary of *Orientalium Dignitas* of Pope Leo XIII (1995). (=OL)

———. *Redemptor Hominis*. Encyclical Letter at the Beginning of His Papal Ministry (1979).

———. *Redemptoris Missio*. Encyclical Letter on the Permanent Validity of the Church's Missionary Mandate (1990).

———. *Vita Consecrata*. Post-synodal Apostolic Exhortation on the Consecrated Life and Its Mission in the Church and in the World (1996). (=VC)

Benedict XVI. *Address to the Inaugural Session of the Fifth General Conference of the Bishops of Latin America and the Caribbean*, Shrine of Aparecida, Sunday, 13 May 2007. (=AA)

———. *Address to the Plenary Assembly of the Congregation for Consecrated Life and Societies of Apostolic Life*, 20 November 2008. (=Plenary CICLSAL)

———. *Africae Munus*. Post-synodal Apostolic Exhortation on the Church in Africa in Service to Reconciliation, Justice and Peace (2011).

———. *Deus Caritas Est*. Encyclical Letter on Christian Love (2005). (=DC)

———. General Audience, 9 April 2008.

———. *Meeting with Catholic Educators*. Address at The Catholic University of America, 17 April 2008.

———. *Spe Salvi*. Encyclical Letter on Christian Hope (2007). (=SS)

Francis. *Address to Participants in the General Chapter of the Salesian Society of St John Bosco*, 31 March 2014.

———. *Address at the Meeting with Seminarians and Novices*, Saturday, 6 July 2013. (=SN)

———. *Address to the Participants at the Plenary Assembly of the International Union of Superiors General*, Rome, 8 May 2013.

———. *Apostolic Letter to all Consecrated People on the Occasion of the Year of Consecrated Life* (2015). (=YCL)

———. *Evangelii Gaudium*. Apostolic Exhortation on the Proclamation of the Gospel in Today's World (2013). (=EG)

———. *Laudato Sì*. Encyclical Letter on Care for Our Common Home (2015). (=LS)

OTHER DOCUMENTS OF THE HOLY SEE

Congregation for Catholic Education. *Consecrated Persons and Their Mission in Schools*. Reflections and Guidelines (2002). (=CPMS)

———. *Lay Catholics in Schools*: Witnesses to Faith (1982). (=LCS)

Congregation for Catholic Education and others. *Presence of the Church in the University and in University Culture* (1994). (=PCU)

Congregation for Institutes of Consecrated Life and Societies of Apostolic Life (=CICLSAL). *Keep Watch! Letter to Consecrated Men and Women Journeying in the Footsteps of God* (2014). (=KW)

———. *Starting Afresh from Christ: A Renewed Commitment to Consecrated Life in the Third Millennium* (2002).

———. *Fraternal Life in Community: 'Congregavit nos in unum Christi amor'* (1994). (=FLC)

———. *Rejoice: A Message from the Teachings of Pope Francis*. A Letter to Consecrated Men and Women in Preparation for the Year Dedicated to Consecrated Life (2014). (= *Rejoice*)

Congregation for Religious and Secular Institutes. *Mutuae Relationes*. Directives for the Mutual Relations between Bishops and Religious in the Church (1978).

———. *Religious and Human Promotion* (Plenaria of the Sacred Congregation for Religious and Secular Institutes, 25–28 April, 1978). (=RHP)

Synod of Bishops. *Message from XIII Ordinary General Assembly of the Synod of Bishops*, 9–28 October 2012 (2012).

OTHER REFERENCES

Constitutions of the Monks of the English Benedictine Congregation. Privately published, 1986; latest edition, 2013. (=EBC Constitutions)

Abbot Bernardo Olivera, OCSO. *Greeting to the Benedictine Abbots' Congress*, Rome 2004. Unpublished, privately circulated.

J Ratzinger. *Christianity and the Crisis of Cultures*. San Francisco: Ignatius Press, 2006.

Antonio Spadaro. 'Wake Up the World: Conversation with Pope Francis about Religious Life'. *Civiltà Cattolica* 165, no. 1 (2014).

Marcus Stock. *Christ at the Centre: Why the Catholic Church Provides Catholic Schools*. Rev. ed. London: Catholic Truth Society, 2012. (=CAC)

INDEX OF REFERENCES TO THE BIBLE AND THE RULE

BIBLE

Exodus	§
33.11	69

Psalms	§
Ps 32	26

Matthew	§
5.15	103
6.19-21	22
7.14	30
7.16-18	104
13.33	104
13.44-46	22
18.20	18
20.28	22
28.19	91

Mark	§
16.15	8

Luke	§
7.8	22
24.17	4
24.26	49
24.31	38
24.32	11
24.33-35	38
24.34	18
24.36-43	129
24.36, 37, 41	38
24.49	47

John	§
3.5-8	41
8.31	70
13–17	51
14.27	102
15.7	70
15.9-10	102
15.14	70
15.15	51
15.16	1, 28, 102
15.18	102
16.4, 8, 13	131
20.22	47

Acts	§
2.1-6	48
2.42-47	41
2.42	18

4.32	18
13.52	45

Romans	§
13.1	22

1 Corinthians	§
10.4	34
10.16	41

2 Corinthians	§
4.7	2
8.9	114
13.13	41

Galatians	§
6.2	56

Ephesians	§
3.7	80
4.13	22

Philippians	§
2.5-11	22, 49
3.8	10

1 Thessalonians	§
1.5	10

2 Thessalonians	§
3.10-12	54

Hebrews	§
12.1-2	87
12.2	79

1 Peter	§
1.22	70

RULE OF ST BENEDICT

Prologue	§
Prol.1	2, 13
Prol.3	19, 82
Prol.6	24
Prol.9	97
Prol.11-12	62
Prol.14	1, 16
Prol.17	84
Prol.19, 20, 21	20
Prol.40-41	24
Prol.45	16, 19
Prol.47	82
Prol.48-49	24
Prol.48	30
Prol.49-50	24
Prol.49	100
Prol.50	50

Chapters of the Rule

	§
1.2	19
1.5	19
1.11	82
2.1	22
2.2	22
2.2, 3	20
2.7	21
2.8, 9	22

2.11	22	23.1	82
2.33-34	109		
2.39	22	27	23
		27.1	22
3	62	27.8	22
3.3	63		
3.7	63	28.2	22
3.8	82		
3.11	109	31.2	23
		31.9	114
4.1-2	80	31.10	86
4.22-26	50	31.17	110
4.29	84		
4.60	82	33.3-4	82
4.73	84	33.4	33
4.75-78	24		
4.78	19	34.5	84
5.7	82	37.1	22
5.10	76		
		39.6	22
7.12, 19	82		
7.34, 35-36	24	46.5	23
7.67	80		
7.70	80	48	109
		48.23	109
9.8	22	48.7	109
		48.8	54
13.12	50	48.24-25	109
20.1, 3, 4	82		
		49.6-8	82
21.1	23	49.9	23
21.3	60		
21.4	23	51.1	65

53.1	112	64.13	22
53.15	114	64.17	22
53.18-20	110	66.7	65
58.7	96	67	65
58.10	96		
58.17	29	68	109
58.20	29		
58.23	30	71	26
58.26-28	30	71.1	36
		71.6-9	50
62.3-4	66	72	7, 19, 26, 78
63.2-3	22	72.5	50
63.12	23	72.6	50
		72.7	50
64.7	22	72.8	21
64.8	22	72.11	1
64.9	22		
64.10	22	73.3	22, 70

THEMATIC INDEX

Numbers refer to paragraph numbers in the text.

Abbot, Abbess, 19, 20–23, 36, 58–63, 135
   abbatial election, 61
affectivity, 40, 80–81
Apostolatus Benedictinorum, 106

Baker, Augustine, 75, 106, 138
baptism, baptized, 1, 8, 12, 23, 25, 120, 137
beauty, 67, 100, 138

chastity, celibate. *See* vows
church, monastic life and
   universal church, 3, 9, 12, 28, 32, 37, 39, 49, 77, 101, 112, 114, 130–31, 135, 136–37
   local church, 115–16, 117, 123
   building, 67
   communion of, 41–43, 46, 47, 48, 69, 70–71, 90–91
   and ecumenism, 120
   mission of, 66, 87, 93, 94, 101, 103, 122–23, 127

   and non-Christian religions, 121
communion, 38–51, 52–57, 77, 87, 90, 102–4
   ecclesial nature of, 41, 43, 87, 90, 115
   experts of, 43n, 101
   kenosis and, 49–51, 105, 118
   monastic (fraternal life in), 7, 18–19, 20, 25, 42, 44–48, 50, 52–57, 77, 81, 90, 92–94
   spirituality of, 7, 18, 43, 45, 62, 65, 101
Congregation, English Benedictine, 9, 87–89
consecration, 6, 8, 11, 12, 31, 37, 52, 85, 92, 94, 95, 100, 111, 132, 137
contemplation (*also see* prayer, personal), 11, 45, 71, 73, 74–76, 83, 117, 136
conversatio morum. See vows
conversion, 79, 82, 112

desire, 28, 45, 107, 125, 133

97

elderly, sick, vulnerable, 55, 56, 60
emotional maturity, 24, 80–81, 85
enclosure, 65–67, 106
Eucharist, 69, 130
evangelical counsels (*also see* vows), 11, 33
evangelical life, 2, 33, 105
evangelisation, 94, 98, 101, 106, 112, 113, 119, 133, 135
  new, 114, 127

formation, 7, 25–27, 89
  initial, 31
  on-going, 40
friendship, 26, 45, 51, 70, 72, 81, 85

good zeal, 7, 19, 26, 50, 78
gospel, 2, 3, 8, 9, 15, 17, 20, 32, 44, 51, 86, 94, 100, 106, 110, 113, 137
growth, integrity, 40, 52, 77–86, 98, 99

habit, religious, 30
holiness, 12, 23, 40, 79, 97, 104
hospitality, 60, 106, 112, 114, 119

inculturation, 113
individualism, 7, 44

joy, 3–5, 24, 38, 44–46, 79, 82, 94, 100, 102, 107, 133

Kingdom of God, 12, 30, 32, 54, 73, 84–85, 113
Koinonia. *See* communion

lectio divina, 70–72, 76, 108, 109, 120
Liturgy of the Hours (= *Opus Dei*), 69, 76, 120, 130–33
love
  God's, Jesus', 2, 3, 21, 24, 43, 80, 81, 86
  for God, Jesus, 8, 15, 24, 85
  in practice, 40, 43, 48, 51, 61, 77, 78, 80, 84, 85
  faith, hope and, 25

martyr, martyrdom, 88, 99–100
  of charity, 118
mission, commission, 8, 46, 48, 61, 73, 87, 94, 98–99, 100, 116, 133
  communion and, 20, 48, 60, 72, 90–91, 101–4
  consecration and, 12, 92, 95, 97
monastery, 7, 8, 67
  administration, 21n, 23, 60
  authority, 22, 23, 60, 64
  consultation, 58, 62–64, 111
  images in Rule, 19

fraternity of, 23, 60
koinonia of, 41–42, 44
sacramental dynamic of, 39, 102
school of Lord's service, 16, 19, 40, 52, 57, 77, 124

obedience, vow of. *See* vows
oblates, lay, 116
officials, 23, 60–61

parishes, pastoral mission, 72, 106–7, 117–19
Paschal Mystery, 16, 24–25, 47
paternity, spiritual, 20, 21–23
peace, peace-making, 38, 47, 84, 102, 129
poor, poverty, 86, 114, 118
poverty
  spirit of, 86, 110
  vow of. *See* vows
prayer, 24, 50, 54, 61, 65, 69, 70, 73, 83, 109, 110, 116, 120, 130,
  personal (*also see* contemplation), 27, 71–72
profession
  baptism and, 1, 6, 8, 120, 137
  clothing and, 30–31
  formation and, 28–32
  and mission of monastic life, 92, 137

vows and, 11, 33–37
prophet, prophecy, 66, 84, 113, 126, 134–38
purity of heart, 40, 52, 70, 76, 80, 83–84, 99

reconciliation, 50, 51, 81, 84, 112, 130
Religiosus Ordo, 106
Rule
  authority of, 9, 22, 58, 63, 78, 80, 96, 135
  discipline of, 82

schools, 72, 106, 112, 122–28
selfishness, self-will, 57, 79, 82
sin, repentance, 3, 79, 80
Spirit, Holy, 9, 10, 20, 21, 23, 26, 38, 39, 41, 43, 44, 45, 62, 68, 76, 80, 81, 83, 85, 90, 95, 131
stability. *See* vows
study, learning, 27, 89, 106, 107, 108, 122

Trinity, 20, 23, 25, 39, 41, 44–46, 64, 74

virtue, 78–79, 82
vocation
  divine call, 1–3, 6, 13–14, 20, 28, 97
  encounter, 11, 15–17, 24, 37

call to communion, 25, 41, 87
call to holiness, 12, 25, 96, 107
prayer and, 70–71
education in, 112, 122, 126, 136

vows
chastity celibate, 33, 37, 85
conversatio morum, 27, 29, 33, 35, 65
obedience, 26, 29, 33, 36, 50, 60, 63, 85, 96, 97
poverty, spirit of, 86, 110
poverty, 33, 85, 86, 121
stability, 29, 33, 34, 65

work, 54, 86, 105–11
overwork, work imbalance, 56, 107–10
underwork, 109

young monks, nuns, 56, 62, 63, 89

www.ingramcontent.com/pod-product-compliance
Lightning Source LLC
Chambersburg PA
CBHW051953290426
44110CB00015B/2227